A
Return
to Italy

By Thomas Perro

A Return to Italy by Thomas Perro

Cover design by Jan Kostka

© by Thomas Perro, 2020

ISBN 978-1-950423-36-1 Paperback
ISBN 978-1-950423-35-4 E-book

Produced by Winged Hussar Publishing, LLC
Under the imprint Wrong Way Books

This book is dedicated to the dreamer/ explorer in all of us!

Fosdinovo

Barga

Massa

Montecarlo

✪ *Florence*

✪ *Pisa*   Poppi

San Miniato

Lari   Certaldo   Anghiari

Livorno San Gimignano

Monteriggioni   *Arezzo*

Volterra   Monte San Savino

Siena   Cortona

Montefollonico

Montepulciano

Campiglia Marittima Suvereto   Montalcino   Pienza

Populonia

✪ *Grosseto*

Sorano

Pitigliano

Tuscany and it's major cities

2

CHAPTER 1
Sono un Italiano!

I am Italian, 100%.

I was born in Brooklyn, New York to parents who were both born in New York City, so that makes me 100% American.

I am a CPA, and numbers have always been my staple. In my world, things are not right unless the numbers work out and balance. The math in my equation is not adding up. How can I be 100% Italian plus 100% American.? That simply does not add up.

The facts are that my heritage is 100% Italian, but my upbringing was 100% American.

Growing up, I knew of my family's origin. Italy was where my family came from. The customs we incorporated into our family traditions were Italian.

History tells us the probable reasons for migration to America. Reportedly, people lived in poverty and there were promises of "The American Dream." Poverty is a poorly defined term. Many people living in poverty do not think that they are poor. The label raises its hideous head when living conditions are compared to others.

The question remains, why would my ancestors leave their birthplace behind to come to America?

Although I am not certain of all the facts, I will attempt to fill in the blanks, knowing what I know about my parents and grandparents.

My grandfather, Enrico (Henry), on my Mom's side was a native Italian. Born and raised in the Marche region of Italy. The Marche region is in central Italy fronting on the Adriatic Sea. A region of mountains and hills, its only pieces of level land are scattered along river valleys and on the Adriatic shore northwest of Ancona. Manufacturing forms the basis of the economy. Agriculture has declined in importance, although the fishing industry remains noble.

Enrico was a mason by trade and followed the demand for his profession to New York City. It was the late 1920's and New York City construction was in high demand as the city was emerging and expanding rapidly.

Other members of Enrico's family had migrated through the port of New Orleans and settled in Mississippi to work on the farms. On one of his visits to his relatives in Mississippi he met Mafalda, my grandmother. Mafalda was a young girl of 13 who came to America with her brother. They settled in Mississippi and found work picking cotton. There was a wave of Italian immigrants who came to the south after the civil war - many of whom were treated like indentured servants.

I never knew anything about her parents, or her heritage in Italy. She used to tell us how she used to get angry when people talked about how bad the slaves were treated, but she said she was treated equally poorly and lived in the same poverty conditions. She was not however owned by the plantation owners, but Italians were treated as second class citizens there. How she wound up there I really don't know. It was something that no one ever talked about. It was a common practice that a lot of family history was

4

buried, especially if it was dark or sad. As if by not talking about it, it did not exist.

When Enrico met Mafalda, he decided he wanted her to be his wife. He was much older than Mafalda, and she was a minor under the control of her family. Although she had no interest in getting married or leaving her family, her brother forced her to accept Enrico's proposal. He felt it was a means of escape of her poverty-stricken life. She however, wanted no part of it. Mafalda finally consented, Enrico got his wife, and took her to New York. She lived her life full of resentment, and it put a terrible strain on their marriage.

Enrico and Mafalda soon had a daughter, Sarah (My Mom). As was common back in the mid 1920's it was a man's world. Enrico worked hard at his trade, and Mafalda worked hard keeping a home and raising their daughter. Enrico slipped into a world of alcoholism and Mafalda became increasingly sad and lonely. Six years later they had a son, Carlo. Enrico passed away from liver complications in the mid 1950's. I was very young, and I have very little personal recollection to add to his story.

My grandmother lived alone after my grandfather died; I enjoyed my time with her and loved her until she died at the age of 76, I was thirty-six. She never remarried. My Mom would always comment how, "people who did not have a good marriage rarely remarried". Italian wisdom? Who knows!

Growing up we always professed to be Italian, but we considered ourselves American. Our heritages simply coexisted. At home our traditions were Italian, but we took that for granted, and did not embrace the depth of what they represented. Grandma spoke Italian and held onto many of the Italian traditions she brought with her to America. One of our traditions was Christmas eve with the cooking of the seven fishes. My Mom carried on that tradition throughout her entire life, not knowing why, and not really concerned that she only prepared about five different types of fish. Keeping the Italian tradition was the thing that was most important for her.

One of Grandma's traditions, and my personal favorite, was her home-made ravioli. As a child I would help her make them, and it was quite a treat to be a part of it. At a time when many people bought "Italian" food in a box or a freezer, Grandma made it fresh. She would take out a large wooden cutting board and her meat grinder, and it was quite a process. She would grind up the meat and made the pasta from scratch. She started by making a volcano of flour with a hollow crater where she would place the eggs. Then she would stir the egg mixture from the inside out of the wall of flour. I was amazed watching her. And she let me help, to a degree. She would make over one hundred at a time. My favorite part was when she had extra dough, she would cut them up and make them into noodles. It seemed very authentic, but remember, she was from Mississippi. To me, this was what being Italian encompassed.

I never really knew the origins of how she came to learn how to make the ravioli. It must have been some form of family tradition passed down from her Mom, and adapted to American products I presumed, but I never found out.

My Dad, Andy was the son of your stereotypical Italian immigrants. His parents came to America in the early 1900's and they only spoke Italian. His Dad, Domenic, spoke some broken English, but Grandma, Nonna as we used to call her didn't. My

6

grandfather was married several times, and I never really knew any of his wives, my step grandmothers.

I think the main reason our heritage was lost was a deliberate act by my Dad.

There were seven siblings in my Dad's family, and he was the youngest, by quite a few years'. His mom died when my he was very young, and he was raised by his older sisters.

When I was young, we were never close to my Dad's parents. I think my Dad was ashamed of his heritage and being considered an immigrant. It was a time when second generation children just wanted to fit in and put aside the "old country" and embrace the new, to create a new life in America.

My parents, Andy and Sarah were married in 1950. My Dad worked very, very, hard hustling and working two jobs to be successful. Growing up his family was poor, so he started working young, and he was not able to get a good education. He worked several jobs trying to advance and make something of himself. He worked full time for the Post Office while making some extra money flipping burgers at night and on the weekends. He got his GED and went to college at night and after lots of late nights and years he graduated with a degree in Accounting. He pursued that career, and eventually started his own Accounting practice. He was a very successful businessman. Still middle class, but successful.

Andy and Sarah had three children. Their first was Bob who was born in 1952. I came along in 1953, an accident perhaps, and my sister Mary Ann was born a few years later in 1956.

While my Dad worked at the Post Office, he always made time for family vacations, and day trips. After he left to pursue his new career in Accounting, he became more focused on building his business. With that came a change in his time priorities.

My Dad loved music, as an enthusiast, not as an artist. He loved to entertain friends and family in his "finished basement". The finished basement was a 1960's, Queens New York, Italian tradition. It was something all young Italian Americans aspired to obtain. Although my brother and I were very young, we helped him finish the basement. Putting up paneling and building a bar. Dad was so proud of that accomplishment and he loved to entertain there.

Friends and family would come over either on a Saturday night, or a special occasion, and my Dad was in his glory with his music playing and serving up Tom Collins' and Gin and Tonics'.

I get my sense of adventure from my Dad. He also instilled his work ethic in me. He felt it was his role to teach us the value of hard work and how to provide for our families. In part, this might have been a result of immigrants who didn't want to be considered "lazy". Success came at a price. His sense of adventure and passion to pursue his dreams took a back seat to providing for his family.

When my brother and I were six and seven my Dad taught us how to play the guitar. He bought a guitar for us to share, and some music books on how to play and read music. He did not know how to play, but he would read our lesson the night before he taught us, and then teach it to us. It worked. We later performed at most of our family functions. My brother would sing, and we performed for our most appreciative relatives.

Music was my passion. It was so much more than just a past-time. I would listen to songs on the radio and figure out how to play them for our repertoire. I began writing at age fifteen, and music was my voice. Although I didn't perform my songs anywhere, I kept writing. It was the sixties and music was a means of voicing rebellion. Against racism, against the Vietnam War, against the "establishment."

I had dreams of touring the country, playing my music in local bars, and earning just enough to pay for my next meal. I wrote songs with my younger cousin Steve, and we played with various musicians, but we never played any gigs. Just a lot of jammin' and having fun.

I told my Dad I wanted to pursue my dream and he demanded that I go to college. Pursuing my hearts passions and musical yearnings was taboo for him. Although in his heart he knew what that was like, he knew that for me to be able to provide for my family I would have to go a different route.

Business College was the absolute last thing I wanted to do.

One of my cousins, Billy who was two years older than me was going to college in Arizona. I thought that was a perfect plan. My Dad squashed that idea, and Billy left for college. When I was eighteen, I compromised and agreed to go to college in New York. My Dad was determined that I should major in business, so I agreed to go to a business college that also had a music degree program.

After my first year in college, I decided music theory was not for me, so I switched to a business major and rationalized that I could go into business, become wealthy, and then pursue my music dreams.

That never happened!

My Dad's sense of adventure surfaced many times in his life. He decided we had to go to Walt Disney World in Orlando, Florida when it first opened in 1971. Bear in mind, there were no superhighways, and it was a four-day trip to get there from where we lived in New York. That didn't stop Dad, he packed the three kids into the family car, with no air-conditioning and we went to Orlando.

It was his fantasy, and we all had a great time, except the part about spending four days in a hot car with two people who thought nothing of smoking in the car with three kids in the back seat. God bless the sixties!

This is where my hypothesis kicks in. I think my dad was ashamed, well that's a little harsh. Let's just say he wanted to be better than an Italian immigrant. He wanted to live the American dream. Through hard work he became a successful American. Italy, or being Italian wasn't part of the equation. He saw it as an obstacle to his plan.

It was a common practice in the 50's that the wife was to be seen and not heard, and my Mom was submissive to my Dad's plans. Although she spoke Italian with her mother, she never spoke a word of it in our house, except some choice swear words when she was upset. As if we didn't know what she was saying. That was our Italian language lesson, learning some choice words when she got angry. She felt that cursing in Italian was just not as bad as cursing in English, which she never did.

Thinking back, as a child in the 60's, I'm not sure how receptive I would have been to learn the Italian language. In America, only immigrants spoke another language – it made you foreign and we were born here. As far as Italian heritage, I had a hard-enough time in school keeping up with American History.

Who's to blame?

Who abandoned my Italian heritage?

I'm afraid we are all to blame, as well as our society. Times were hard for middle class kids. Lots of racism in the 60's. Not against Italians, but it still seemed there was a battle to be good Americans.

Italian? That's what my grandparents were.

As for me, I was an American!

Before my adventure began, I was truly 100% American. I've since learned that it's not enough to be an American.

I have a heritage. I am part of something much bigger than that.

Not because I choose to be, but because I am undeniable a part of the Italian culture. These are my roots, and this is something that I must find out about. Not because I dislike being an American, or because I think I should go back to my roots, but because this is the very core of my being an Italian.

As I grew older and continued my pursuit of the American dream of being a successful businessman with a large house in the suburbs, I never gave my heritage a thought.

It wasn't until later, after my children got married and left the house that I began the pursuit of my Italian heritage.

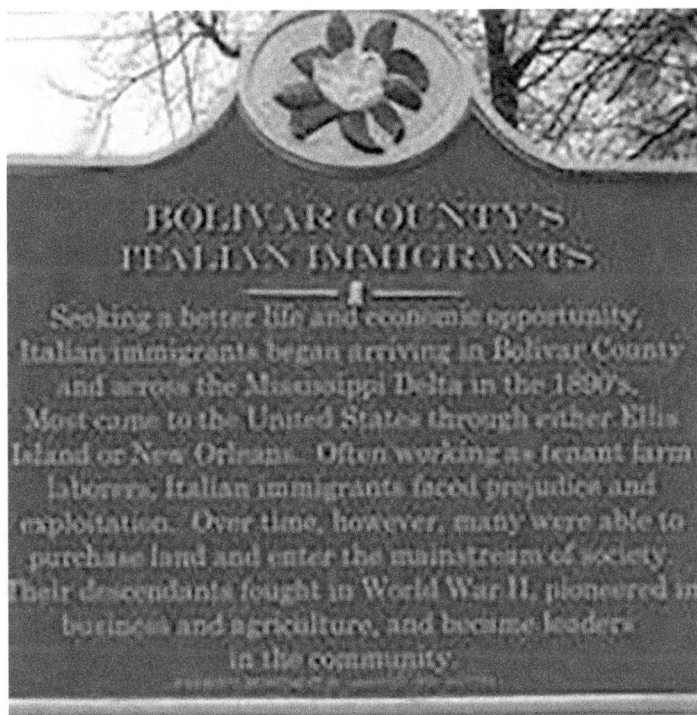

A marker remembering Italians in Mississippi

CHAPTER 2
La creazione!

I met my wife Fern in 1970. I was seventeen and it was love at first sight. We met at work. When I first saw her in the lunch-room I told my co-worker buddy that one day I could marry her. Little did I know that she was going to be the woman I would spend the rest of my life with.

We were married in 1974. We had three children, Tom, who came as quite a surprise in 1975, Mike in 1978 and then our daughter Jaime in 1981.

Nobody believed us when Tom came eight months after our wedding, but it was true, he was conceived on our wedding night, and he was born one month premature. Two virgins experimenting in the sexual world. Who knew we were so fertile?

My wife was half Italian. Fern's Dad, Mike was the son of Italian immigrants, and he looked and spoke like a genuine Italian. Her Mom Lillian, Lil, was a blend of several European nationalities including French, German and English.

I was barely twenty-one when we were married, Fern was a little older at twenty-three. We dated for two years and we just loved to be with each other. We used to spend the evenings sitting in my car by the water talking until the wee hours of the morning. There was a little kissing, but it never went any further than that. After the make out portion we would just talk about dreams and how wonderful our life would be together, forever.

Fern's youngest brother Bruce was two years younger than me and we shared the same interest in music. Some dates, Fern and I would go back to her house and watch TV with her family. Her Mom and Dad would go to bed early, and Fern and I would just sit on the couch and continue to watch TV. When Bruce was home, he and I would laugh and talk about the upcoming bands in Rock, and Fern often wondered if he was the reason I liked to stay so long.

Of course, when I went home early in the morning after our dates my Mom did not believe a word of what I said we were doing.

Fern and I thought it made sense to get married. Her Mom and Dad had an apartment in their basement that was not being used, and we just wanted to be together, all the time.

Our wedding plans were simple, and for me was just a means for us to continue our dream. My brother was also planning to get married. Being the first born he felt he should be the first to get married. Fern and I were young, innocent and foolish, and we did not share that philosophy.

We were married in July, and my brother got married in November. Looking back, I realize how inconsiderate and foolish that was for us to do that.

I was in my senior year in college, and Fern was working full time. With the reduced rent we were paying, the plan was a good one. During our honeymoon Fern started feeling ill. After we came home, we found out that she was expecting. I did not take that news well. Physically, Fern did not take to pregnancy, and she quit her job a month later. We had no health insurance to pay for the baby, and only my part-time income to live on while

I finished school.

I graduated that June, and got a good job in Accounting, and it looked like things were going to be okay after all.

Fern had a different upbringing than I did, and we did not share the same work ethic. She felt alone at home single handedly raising a child and she thought I should be there to share that burden. I was, but I also had to pursue my career and work my way up the corporate ladder. She did not agree. She would beg me to call out sick and stay home with her. I had a responsibility to my job, and I had a limited amount of sick days. Again, she did not share those priorities. One day she was not winning the argument for me to stay home so she hid my shoes. In the financial condition we were in I only owned one pair of shoes, so that was a day to remember. We joked about it in later years, but it was not very funny at the time.

In the meantime, I was still actively trying to pursue my music. My cousin and I were still writing and playing, but with a new baby, Fern had no patience for that.

We were young, and foolish and made so many bad decisions. Financially, it took twenty-five years to finally recover.

During those tumultuous times is when God reached into my life and grabbed hold of me.

I was raised Roman Catholic. Went to Parochial school for twelve years, was an altar boy, and received all the Sacraments. I always felt drawn to God, but I never found the fulfillment I was looking for in the Church. I was content to know that God was real, that I could talk to him in prayer, and life was okay without any more interference from Him.

I was so wrong.

It was 1985 and I was unemployed.

When the Company I was working at, for over six years was sold, I opted for an exit package. I had my degree, some experience, and my CPA and I wanted to start my own firm and become an entrepreneur. Even though I was asked to stay, I opted for the exit deal.

Ultimately, that was the right decision, but it took ten years to become a reality.

In the meantime, I was working as a delivery driver. Using my car, I would deliver small articles to local clients on my route. The commissions I made barely made up for the gas I spent making the deliveries.

It was during this time that God got my attention. As a lover of music, I considered myself a "Rocker." I was always listening to rock music on the radio while I drove. One day I was compelled to search the radio for a different station. I found a Christian talk radio station. I listened. After the program ended, I was so moved that I pulled the car over and wept!

I don't recall the message, but what I heard made my heart yearn to learn more about God.

When I got home, I told Fern about it. She was not interested because she had always wanted us to go to church, and I never had the desire to go. She was angry and resentful that now I said it was time to go.

So, my Son Tommy, who was now ten, and I set off to find a good Bible-teaching Christian Church. We visited different churches each Sunday until we found one that seemed to be the right fit.

At first, it was only me and Tommy who attended Church regularly. It was a Baptist Church and they had three services per week. As a Catholic, I was shocked that we had to go to church three times per week. But I found that I couldn't wait till the next Service. I was learning so much about God through the Bible, and I couldn't get enough of it.

During my years as a Catholic I never read or even owned a Bible. I thought that was something that only Priests could have.

I learned that it was not enough to know **about** God, but that I needed to *know* God. Soon over time, I learned more about what that meant and one-day I accepted Jesus Christ as my Lord and Savior. I have to admit, I did not fully comprehend that completely right away, but I was learning more and more about it every day.

To my Roman Catholic family and friends, I was an outcast! I tried to explain to them what that meant, but I failed miserably.

In the Bible, Jesus said, "I am the way, the truth and the life: no man comes to the Father but by me." (John 14:6) "Come to the Father" means we get to spend eternity in Heaven with God.

The most popular Bible verse that describes this is John 3:16 which states, "For God so loved the world that He sent his only begotten Son, that whoever believes in Him shall not perish but have eternal life."

This simply means that you have to call on Jesus, personally. All you have to do is say something like this, "God, I know that I am a sinner, and I know that I've done wrong in my life. The best I know how, I turn from my sin and I turn to You, by

17

faith. Come into my heart, and my life and save me, and forgive me. Oh, Jesus, I believe You died on the Cross for me. I believe You shed your blood for me. Today, I trust in You and place my faith in You as my Savior." If you said that in your heart and meant it, you are born-again! It's as simple as that!

A few months after I was going to Church regularly Fern came to one of the Church's Easter Musical dramas. She was struck by God with the same truths that I had learned. She accepted and started to attend regularly with me.

Then something amazing happened. God put music back into my life. I got involved with several musicians at the church. I played and led the music during the Sunday evening services. I formed a band with my son Tom, and we played several Christian coffee houses which were a big hit during that time.

I have been playing in bands, and leading worship services ever since. I even got to display some of my talent playing saxophone solo's at Church.

I wrote, produced and directed annual Easter musical dramas consisting of large choirs, several soloists, and several actors for over ten years.

Everything I ever dreamt for musically was totally fulfilled, and I am so thankful that God gave that to me.

Back to my story. It was now 2010, our children were all grown, married and out on their own. I felt it was time. Time to begin to travel.

I planned our first adventure. We were going to Europe. We asked our two friends Steve and Katy if they wanted to join us. We had previously traveled to Hawaii together, so they passed the litmus test of being compatible travel partners.

It was a cruise starting in Venice and cruising down the Adriatic to several ports including some Greek islands and Turkey.

Being the planner of the excursion, I decided that since we already paid for airfare to get to Italy, why not see a little bit of it. We flew into Rome and did the tourist thing. Rushed off to see the Vatican, the Spanish steps, the Coliseum and on and on for three days. The architecture and history were amazing! Trying to picture what it must have been like back in the day when the city was a part of everyday life. We were simply American tourists in Italy. Something about it just didn't feel right.

I began to think what it must be like to actually live there.

To be a part of that Italian culture. To stop and talk to people on the street walking to the market, in no rush to get there, but more interested in connecting with friends and neighbors. To sit and sip a coffee with neighbors for hours with no concern for time passing or having to be somewhere. This is the Italian way. Relationships, friendships, being friendly, sociable unintentionally, all of which just came naturally to the Italians people.

After a few days in Rome, we picked up a train to Florence. Florence is a city in central Italy and it is the capital city of the Tuscany region. Traveling by rail is the best means of travel in Europe, but for four American tourists with lots of luggage and no knowledge of the language, it was far from enjoyable. What track, which train, where do we put all of our luggage, where do we sit, where do we get off? It was very stressful, and the utter joy of traveling through the countryside was lost in translation for us.

We were American tourists, on a mission. To get to Florence to be on vacation. To just slow down and enjoy the journey was not even a consideration.

In Florence we remained very busy sightseeing. Busy, busy, busy. Rushing from church to church, museum to museum, grabbing quick bites at tourist traps, trying to take in hundreds of years of history and culture in a few days. We had our work cut out for us.

We did take a cooking class where they took us to the market to buy the ingredients we needed for our class. We made homemade pasta, Caprese salad, and tiramisu. It was so much fun, and the food tasted amazing.

But more than that, I saw some of what life there might really be like. My heart was stirring, I was being drawn into the Italian lifestyle and heritage. Yet, we remained American tourists in Italy, trying to get it all in.

We rented a car in Florence to drive to Venice for our cruise. I drove, Steve was the navigator, and it was surprisingly easy to navigate the roads and the hurried Italian drivers who feel that traffic signs are merely a suggestion.

On the way to Venice we stopped at Pisa for about an hour. I had no expectations for seeing this leaning tower but something about it was magical, almost mystical. An air of greatness, beauty, accomplishment. I felt such a fulfillment in seeing the tower that my heart skipped a beat. I can't explain it, other than I felt the heart of the country right there. I was awestruck, and just sat there and stared at the tower, and the people milling around. I began to feel the magic of Italy, right there.

It was time to go, so we jumped in the car and continued our trek to Venice.

Venice was another magical place. Walking the streets and canals was amazing, quaint, romantic, peaceful. So full of culture and life, shops displaying their wares, and local authentic food for the taking. Of course, the shop owners make their living from tourism, but it was different. You felt a sense of their pride in their shops and could see some of their heritage in what they made and were selling. We stopped in a shop admiring models of Gondola's. The owner was an old gentleman, who began telling us the history of the Gondola, and said he made them by hand. He asked us if we would like him to make one for us. We said, "Absolutely", and he told us to come back the next day to pick it up. That Gondola sits in my office to this day. I cherish it.

We saw the places of interest, the squares, the churches. We sampled some of the "fishy" foods at some of the local restaurants. But Venice was so much more to me. It touched my heart. I couldn't explain it. That same feeling, I had when I first laid my eyes on my wife. I knew she was my future. In a sense, so was Italy.

Plus, the Gelato was amazing everywhere.

We stayed in Venice for a few days and then we embarked on our cruise.

We thoroughly enjoyed our trip and loved all the sights we were able to see; however, we did not interact with any Italian's other than merchants and waiters.

There was one exception. In Tuscany we took a tour of a vineyard, and our tour guide took a liking to us. He was a young, handsome Italian man in his mid-twenties. He shared a lot about the Italian culture, and their way of life. He was not in a rush to get us to our destination, nor to get us through the tour and go on to the next group. Fern kept remarking how good-looking he was! Hmmm!

Although I didn't realize it at the time, he was displaying some of the traits that makes Italy such a special place. He was sharing his heart, his family, his heritage. The joy of sharing their heritage with foreigners is what makes Italians so endearing and welcoming. Creating such a feeling of warmth and kindness. That magnetism was drawing me. Stirring my heart. Awaking emotions that I never knew existed. I wasn't a tourist anymore, I was home.

I went away feeling that we visited Italy, but we did not visit the Italians. Something in my heart kept saying, "You have to go back!"

In 2014 my wife was diagnosed with kidney cancer. They removed one of her kidney's and put her on a chemo prescription. It seemed to be working with minimal side effects. In the spring of 2015, she said she felt well enough to go back to Italy.

I started the planning process. Our traveling companions could not join us, but we decided to go anyway. I decided, "no sightseeing." We agreed to just observe the people and enjoy the culture.

We combined our trip with a cruise. This time around the Mediterranean.

One of our ports was Naples, and we hired a taxi driver to take us around the city. He asked us if we wanted to go to Pompei. Fern was feeling very sluggish, and we did not want to do anything so strenuous. We told him that we weren't really interested, and he said it was like going to Rome and not seeing the Pope!

We went.

Throughout the trip he talked about his people, his family, and showed us a more personal side of Italy. He even sang along with "That's Amore" a Dean Martin classic in his car for us. That was the highlight of the trip for Fern.

He told us about how he felt that people in Naples were more laid back than the people in Rome.

He told us how important it was that they all gathered around the television on Sunday afternoons to watch the football (Soccer) games.

He loved telling us about his city, his family, and their traditions.

We asked him to drop us off at one of the restaurants that he and his family ate at, no tourists. What a different dynamic. Great food, and great interaction with the staff.

Getting that feeling again. That different feeling about being in Italy. About being amongst Italian people. Observing and absorbing their culture and ways of life.

We finished our cruise in Rome and we spent three days just walking around, observing the Italian people. People-watching, eavesdropping on conversations in cafés.

This is what I had been searching for. I just didn't know it.

Fields in the Campagna

CHAPTER 3
Un uomo grasso!

Soon after we returned from our trip, I lost my partner in life, my best friend. My wife Fern passed away after a relatively short battle with kidney cancer. I never realized how much she meant to me until after she was gone. I thought we would have so much more time to live our dreams, more time to just hold each other and dance.

I grieved a lot harder than I expected. I was emotionally devastated, but I was still able to function.

That was the hardest year of my life. I was constantly working through my grief, trying to find that new normal for me. It had totally consumed me. I was angry because I felt that all the counsel I received, through the many books I read and my private counselling sessions, were attempting to make me forget Fern and move on. This was not the case at all. What I discovered toward the end of that year was that I had to process my grief in stages. The stages followed no pattern or order and varied in intensity each time they arose. I had so many issues to work through. At age twenty-one. I went directly from living in my parents' home to being married. I never experienced living alone as a bachelor.

At social functions I always took a back-seat allowing Fern to shine. Fern was always the life of the party and I always felt that I was just Fern's husband. Now I had to find my identity. I had to find out who "Tom" was, without Fern.

One morning as I was praying, I had an epiphany. A revelation of a sort. I felt the presence of God. It was almost as if I could hear him audibly. I could not, but it was a surreal experience. The message was that I had to suffer through this grief. It was a time of growth and understanding for me, and that I was going to come out of it a stronger person. What I heard was God telling me that He was not going to get me out of this, but that He was going to get me through this. And although it was a very, very, lonely time, I received His assurance that He was always there with me. That He had been with me throughout this whole experience with His arms wrapped around me, holding me tight, and that He was going to continue to be there to comfort me and help me grow in my faith.

After this revelation, I realized that I had to move on, but not in the way that I thought. My relationship with Fern was what I had to let go of. The relationship I had with Fern had to change. Although she would always be a part of my life, she had to become a fond memory. A memory of times gone by.

A year after I lost Fern, I thought I might enjoy a couple of weeks in Tuscany. I wanted to return to a place I could feel calm. A distant place that looked nothing like home and did not remind me of my life. I thought it would be a time of refreshment and cleansing. A fresh start so to speak.

I did not want to go to see any sights, or even to see the world, but I hungered to see my life in a different light.

I wanted to live amongst the people. Eat with them, drink wine with them, talk with them, learn from them. I thought it would also be a good opportunity to get back my heritage. To learn about my grandparents, indirectly by learning about the Italian people. I decided to go to Tuscany because when I was there, I felt the Italian warmth. The Italian hospitality. The heart of the Italian people was certain to be found there in Tuscany.

Yes, I was going to do it.

I bought some books on Tuscany to help me in planning my journey, my quest. One of the books was about a similar journey taken by the author. His quest was to live with the Italian people too. The way he accomplished this was by volunteering to work on farms in Italy. This is called WOOFING.

WWOOF is an acronym for the World-Wide Organization of Organic Farmers. Farms post their farms and their needs with this organization, and people can work on the farm in exchange for room and board.

This sounded very interesting, and the more I investigated it the more appealing it became. Turns out, in most cases, you stay with the family who owns the farm, eat with them, and work side by side with them in the fields. This sounded like the perfect solution to the quest I was about to embark on.

I joined the Italian regional branch of the organization and searched hundreds of farm profiles to see which was the best fit for me.

Now, a little about me. I was sixty-two, overweight, and quite out of shape. I am a CPA, and my work life revolves around sitting all day at a desk behind a computer. After working all day, to have a meal and sit in front of the television until it was time to go to bed was my norm. My physical prowess left a little to be desired.

In constructing my profile for the organization, I thought it best to make sure I painted a clear picture of who I was before

I came prancing through the door greeting these farmers. My fear was that the farmers would be expecting a young, fit farm worker, and be quite surprised when I arrived, a fat, unfit old man.

The method of connecting with the farmers is through email.

Wow, technology even on a farm.

I sent emails to about fifty farms that seemed to be a good fit in the Tuscany area. What I read, was that the farms would be slow to respond if they did at all.

I was planning a three-week adventure, and I had hoped to work on three different farms to get some different perspectives. Turns out most farmers require a two-week minimum.

I guess I overlooked that very important piece of information.

One farm responded to me and as expected, said that they required a two-week minimum. I quickly responded that I could do two weeks, and their response was, "ok then come."

Since they were slow to respond, that back and forth communication took two weeks. Lots of anxiety on my part because I had already bought my non-refundable airline tickets.

I now had two weeks covered and I felt good about the trip, which was still two months away. I just needed one more farm, but who will take me for one week? I offered my services to the farm that said "ok" and they said they could not use me the third week.

I sent more emails to my "B" list of farms.

Wait . . . Wait . . . Wait . . .

I received an email, but it was from the farm that accepted my offer telling me they didn't need me. I flipped out, but the

28

only thing I could do was to email her back. After a few more emails she then confirmed that It was ok for me to work with them.

Wait . . . Wait . . . Wait . . .

I received a very favorable response from a farmer who was very excited to have me come and work on his farm, and he said one week would be fine.

All set!

I planned my trip mid-October because I wanted to experience the harvesting of grapes and olives. Possibly to be involved in the making of the wine and olive oil.

Now a little bit about the volunteer profile. Volunteers work Monday through Friday, six hours per day, weekends off. Room and board are provided by the farmers, and volunteers can stay on the weekend at no charge. There are about 20,000 WWOOFR's worldwide ranging from age twenty-one to thirty-five. It appeared to me that I might be the old man on the farm after all.

Sounded great, but what was I going to do to be able to work for more than ten minutes without having a heart attack? This was a real problem.

I decided I should start working out on the treadmill and lose at least twenty pounds in preparation for the trip. After trying that for a week, and not being very successful, I realized I needed some motivation.

One of my friends recommended a ten-week program with daily aerobics classes and nutritional assistance. I inquired and decided that was NOT going to be the right course of action for me. I decided to join a gym and work with a trainer. The gym I went to also had daily classes and I thought that I had found the perfect solution.

I worked on the treadmill every day for a week, but was unable to get a trainer, and the classes they had were either too advanced, or Zumba which is more like dancing.

Not for me.

Now, what was I going to do?

In the meantime, I had received an email from one of the challenges' I spoke to previously saying they were starting the ten-week program the following Monday.

I called them, visited the class, and signed up.

Five weeks before I leave for Italy. Could I do this?

Sounded like a plan!

When I arrived at my first class, I was shocked and disappointed to see that my instructor was not a bikini-clad perfect specimen of a woman. The instructor looked a lot like just one of us.

To my surprise she was very capable of leading the class, and I barely made it through the stretching exercises.

I hung in there for the entire forty-minute workout. Stopping many times to catch my breath and struggling through many exercises at my own slower pace. Snail's pace that is.

I had been dieting fairly consistently so I was now down seven pounds going into the challenge, and I was feeling a little more confident that I was going to be able to do this.

I finished my first week strong. Attended every class, and no cheating on the diet. I felt good, but I didn't lose one pound more.

Frustrated I continued my program.

The second week was much better. I almost made it through the entire class without stopping to catch my breath . . . almost!

Finally, on Saturday morning I weighed in at a three-pound loss for the week.

Down ten, ten to go.

I continued for the entire four weeks, was finally able to touch my toes, and I was down thirteen pounds. I was still disappointed in the weight loss but was very happy about my strength and stamina.

I came to terms with the fact that I was about as physically fit as I was going to be.

Turn of the century schoolroom

CHAPTER 4
Non parlo Italiano!

The owners at both of the farms I was planning to work on all spoke English, but Italian was still their primary language.

As I said, we never learned to speak Italian at home, and the few words I did know might get me in trouble. I did not want to have that elitist American attitude that people all over the world should speak English to accommodate me. I decided I would have to learn to speak some Italian. It was something I had always thought about, and this seemed as good a time as any.

My goal was to master the Italian language in two-months. I really thought that it was possible. I purchased a language program book with an audio CD. The further I studied the more confident I was that I was NOT going to accomplish my goal.

I made flash cards and continued my lessons. I didn't realize just how difficult this task was going to be. I thought it would be easier to learn Italian because I was older, and I had heard it when I was younger.

I felt so ridiculously stupid. I wondered, "How did I ever get this far in life being so stupid?" Aiuto!

I heard that if I watched Italian movies with English sub-titles, I could pick up some Italian. I tried that, but the one movie I watched was very interesting, and halfway through watching the movie I forgot to listen and learn the language. I got so caught up in the plot I just read through and watched the entire movie. It turned out to be a pretty good movie. I didn't learn anything.

Feeling desperate I decided to see if I could find a tutor. As it turns out, there is a network of language tutors online. Most of the tutors wanted to work online, but I really wanted live lessons. I connected with a tutor, Helen, who was local, and we met at a local library which was very close to my home.

Helen had a South African accent, which took me by surprise. I asked her if she had an accent when she spoke Italian. She chuckled and said no.

What do I know?

My first lesson went very well so I decided it was a good idea to continue. As I progressed, I was happy that I was able to actually memorize some things. I deduced that at my age, you just started forgetting things, and had no need to learn new things.

I continued with my lessons, but about a week before my trip I had a meltdown at my tutoring session. My mind went blank and I just shut down. I continued to study on my own, but I never regained my confidence.

Up until now, I was so focused in preparing for the trip I didn't have time to think about other things. Upon losing my wife after forty-one years; after spending my whole life caring for my wife and my family. I was about to do something all alone.

I thought I had experienced all that life had to offer. I thought I had completed my journey.

God had different plans. He brought me through the pain of losing my wife and wanted to continue teaching me. After many years, I finally started to learn about becoming a man. A man full of emotions and adventure.

I had finally begun my journey to become a person capable of feeling people's pain and suffering. I began to understand what it was like to be lonely, and at times, even hopeless.

My journey, which started just a few months prior, would now become my next chapter.

Olive trees in Tuscany

Chapter 5
Incredibile!

Day one of my journey arrived. It was Saturday October 15, 2016.

How naïve of me to think that flying to a foreign country thousands of miles away by myself would be without complications or fear.

I was so excited about the trip.

I was packed and ready to go by nine a.m., but the car service wasn't picking me up until one-thirty because my flight wasn't until six-fifteen.

I was a little anxious.

I had access to a VIP lounge at the airport through the new credit card that I got. The lounge advertised that they offered a comfortable environment with free food and beverages, so I thought, why not just go early. I called the car service and asked if they could come an hour early, which they were able to do.

The driver was a delightful gentleman from the Dominican Republic. We had a very pleasant conversation and drive to the airport. It was a beautiful, sunny fall day perfect for a drive.

He dropped me at the terminal, and there were not a lot of people there. That had me wondering if maybe I was at the wrong terminal.

It has happened to me before.

I made my way up to the counter to check my bag. Right terminal, wrong time. It was one-fifteen and since my flight wasn't until six-fifteen the woman at the counter said I could not check my bag until two.

I found a chair and read for a bit.

Time passed rather quickly, until I was able to check my bag and proceed to the lounge.

I went through security rather quickly and found the lounge. Turns out there are several VIP lounges and the one I was eligible for was before the security checkpoint, so I had to go back out to the terminal and find the lounge.

It was nice, comfy seats and couches, open bar, some sandwiches and light snacks. It was not the ultimate buffet I had hoped for, but it was nice enough.

Being the careful traveler that I am I thought I should head to the gate a little early as I had to go through security again. It took me about ten minutes to get through the security checkpoint and I arrived at the gate an hour before boarding time.

No big deal.

I read a few more chapters in my book which was finally getting interesting.

Boarding time arrived! But no boarding announcements.

Then the announcement came that there were mechanical issues and our flight was going to be delayed.

Not a very comforting thought.

The announcements kept coming, and the delay became longer. No big deal, I thought, except that I had a connecting flight in Amsterdam with only a one-hour layover.

I feared that was an issue when I booked the flight, but the airline ticket agent assured me that there was another flight that I could get on in case I missed my connection.

We finally boarded and took off two hours late, I received an email from the airline indicated that I was going to miss my connection and they booked me on the next available flight.

Just as a side note, in this age of modern technology the cell phone service has not kept up with the idea of making travel effortless. They offered me several options and plans for my international stay, none of which were easy to understand or inexpensive.

The fear of God, or the fear of my next phone bill set in.

Airplane mode, shut off data, find Wi-Fi, these were the challenges for fear of doing the wrong thing and getting hit with exuberant charges on my telephone bill.

The flight was packed, and the conversations of most passengers were their anxiety of what they were going to do about connecting flights.

I read a little, and slept a little, until we landed.

Welcome to Amsterdam!

The airline crew assured everyone that there would be staff waiting at the gate to help us with our connections. That was a half-truth because there was one attendant, yes one person to help all of these frantic travelers. The attendant proceeded to tell me that I missed my flight and that I would have to go to the transfer desk to get a boarding pass.

I followed the crowd to the transfer desk.

Turns out they wanted everyone to go to the self-help kiosk and figure it out themselves.

I input my boarding pass and "lo and behold" it printed out my new boarding pass.

Sweet, I really was booked on the next flight.

It was now ten a.m. and my car rental agreement was for me to pick up my car at eleven. I knew this was going to be a problem.

I looked at my boarding pass and it said boarding time was fourteen-twenty-five. Everything in Europe is military time so I kept having to do the math.

Oh my, that's two-twenty-five!

I reached out to an agent who was standing by, helping frantic travelers who were being diverted to different cities to reach their final destination. I asked if there was an earlier flight and she said I was very lucky to have gotten that flight, most people were not connecting until later that evening.

I did not feel very lucky but, oh well time to find another VIP lounge.

Amsterdam is a very big airport and there were several lounges, each of which were on different sides of the airport. I had plenty of time, so I strolled through the airport observing the different type of people walking through the airport. I could tell I was not in New Jersey.

I made it to the lounge, lounge fifty-one, only to be informed I was to go to lounge four-twenty-one down the corridor up one flight by the Starbucks. I was not surprised to find that there was a Starbucks! Some things are the same no matter where you are.

Halfway down the corridor I stopped and asked someone if I was going in the right direction. I was, just go to the Starbucks and take the elevator.

Starbucks, of course!

I found the Starbucks and the elevator but there were two lounges forty and forty-one.

I went into forty and the woman at the counter said I was in the wrong lounge. I asked about lounge four-twenty-one and she gave me a very puzzled look. Then I realized that four-twenty-one was forty-one with a very strong German accent.

I repeated to myself four-twenty-one, four-twenty-one, four-tee-one, oh yeah forty-one.

Lounge forty-one was correct, and the receptionist said I was in the right place until she saw I was going to Florence at which time she said I was in the wrong lounge. She told me I had to go through Passport control to lounge twenty-six.

Back to the terminal.

She was right and I found lounge twenty-six. It was eleven AM and my flight was at three PM. Sorry fifteen hundred!

I emailed Tina, my farm owner, and explained my dilemma and that I would not be arriving until seven pm. She emailed me back and said, "okay", and that she was looking forward to seeing me tomorrow morning at seven.

Darn military time.

I emailed her back and told her I would be arriving at nineteen hundred and she understood that.

I had some snacks and took a little nap.

The flight was overbooked but that didn't faze me. Turns out, they gave me the emergency exit seat which had additional leg room. It was an hour and a half flight, so I took another nap.

The flight arrived ten minutes early.

When I got on the shuttle to the car rental facility it hit me.

What the heck was I thinking?

I'm all alone in a foreign country!

I don't speak the language!

Fear and anxiety set in!

I was renting a car and traveling one hundred twenty kilometers to a farm on highways whose names I couldn't even pronounce, and it was going to be dark soon.

I printed directions on google maps before I left and had my Garmin navigation system with me (GPS). I was set to go, off to Micciano.

Of course, there were two different ways to get there, so I asked the car rental agent which was the better route. He explained one was more scenic, the other more highway.

I wanted to just cruise the countryside, and enjoy the hills, and vineyards, but it was getting dark, I was in a foreign country with signs in Italian, and no idea if my GPS was going to do the right thing by me.

I was able to locate my car in the rental parking lot.

I tried to follow his directions out to the main road where my GPS would pick up. Not so easy, and my GPS wanted to take me to the highway route. I tried to get off and find my way to the other route. I couldn't do it, so I adhered to the wisdom of the GPS.

Italian people are known for their hospitality and laid-back attitude. But not on the road!

It's not the same as in the United States though, where road rage abounds. The Italian people just seem to be in a hurry on the highway. Nobody is angry, no shouting or giving hand gestures, they just want you to get out of their way. And they never honk their horns. Never!

My GPS was perfect with the directions, but it was rather funny listening to the GPS' very American voice trying to pronounce the Italian street names. She wasn't very good at it.

Everything was going well, although it was now getting dark. I had to get off the highway and it was comforting to see everyone was going the same direction as me. Surprisingly, there were a lot of roundabouts on the road. I thought roundabouts were a New Jersey thing.

The sky darkened, and before I knew it, the road was pitch black. I was trailing a car and suddenly he turned off the road. The road became very winding and I felt like I was the only person on the road. I felt I was the only person in the world. I was expecting to see Rod Serling from the "Twilight Zone" appear in the road in front of me telling me about the signpost up ahead!

At times, I was glad it was dark. That way I could not see what was on the other side of the road barrier, or how close I was to the edge of a cliff.

I was getting close, according to my GPS which I was relying on 100%. I thought, I feared, what if my GPS failed me?

On a dark desolate road all by myself. I thought to myself, "Is this how it ends?" There were no lights, no traffic, just dark, no sounds and lots of stars.

Then I remembered the email from Tina, the farm owner. She told me that the GPS would take me to a deserted road unless I followed the signs to Micciano. Oh boy!

The GPS followed her advice and my GPS was agreeing with her directions.

Then it happened! My greatest fear!

My GPS said, "You have arrived at your destination."

Really?

Had I arrived?

I was on a one lane winding country road in the middle of fields and trees.

I stopped to look around. There was nothing there. I couldn't see anything outside of my headlights in the car. It was very disorienting.

I drove a little further and thought, in the midst of my panic, that I should probably head back to the small town I just drove through and call Tina.

Cell phone panic set in again.

Then the headlights of a car pulled up behind me. I got out of the car to ask them if they knew of the farm I was going to.

It felt like midnight, but it was only around seven-thirty (nineteen thirty).

In the car was an older couple who appeared to be returning home from dinner. They were dressed quite nicely. He in a suit and she in a dress.

I asked them if they knew of my farm. They nodded and started talking to me in Italian.

I said, "non parlo Italiano." They smiled and kept talking to me in Italian. This went on for a little while. They pointed me in a direction, waved and left.

The only thing I understood was that the farm was in fact two kilometers further down the road. Might as well have been a thousand to me at that moment.

I drove two kilometers, and there was nothing. And I mean nothing! I slowed down waiting for the farm to magically appear.

I drove a little further and finally, there it was! I pulled into a driveway and there were cars there, so I felt very relieved.

Tina came out to meet me and she was so very sweet, and I felt I was home. Tina was a woman in her early fifties. She looked Italian, but she didn't look like a farmer. She was well dressed. Casual but nice, and her hair and makeup were of just the right proportion.

She introduced me to my fellow WWOOF'r Jonathan who showed me to our cabin.

Jonathan looked like your typical Midwest college kid. Fair skinned, blonde hair, small and thin. Full of energy and always smiling.

We shared a cabin and we each had our own bedroom. The cabin was very nice. It had a central room when you entered which was a kitchen of sorts. There was a large dining table, a sink, an old stove, and a refrigerator. To the left was one-bedroom, which Jonathan occupied and to the right was another bedroom, which was going to be mine. There was a large bathroom off the main room with a large shower. That was a relief, as showers in Italy are not usually a main concern for guests and are sometimes very small.

I felt very fortunate to have selected Tina's farm. Some farms offer only a barn with no heat or running water for accommodations.

Jonathan was a second-year college student from Colorado, and this was his second week with Tina. He had taken a semester off from college to travel Italy. He was on a limited budget, so woofing enabled him to accomplish this task for the entire summer. He had planned to take the final two weeks of his journey to sightsee.

Tina called us for dinner, and we raced to the main facility of the farm. It was nine PM, which is typically the hour for dinner. Italians would typically eat dinner between seven and ten PM.

The farm is an "Agriturismo", which is a working farm that accommodates guests for a weekly stay of vacationing. Breakfast and dinner are included, both of which are prepared by Tina each day. There was a small pool for guests, and our cabin is rented out during the season.

Tina and Paolo's establishment is more than just a working farm – in addition to producing olives, olive oil, grapes and wine, they also have a restaurant and inn on their premises. It is a small family run business started in the 1950's with seventy hectares of fields, woods and its ancient house dating from 1750. The current farm has been run as a business since 2001 when Tina and Paolo restored the old house creating a farmhouse for agritourism.

The main building was a square brick building surrounded by shrubs and olive trees. There was a small lobby when you entered which opened into the common area. There were large tables in the main room for guests to dine. To the right was a living room with couches and chairs and a television and a fireplace. To the right of that was the kitchen. It was a commercial kitchen as Tina would have to cook for several guests in the height of the tourism season.

The décor was rustic, but very clean.

Upstairs were Tina and Paolo's living quarters, and two suites for guests.

When I first entered the guest dining area there was laundry all over the room. Tina apologized and told me she was doing laundry and had not had a chance to finish. Clothes were hanging all about the room. On drying racks, folded on the table, and hanging over the chairs.

I realized that this truly was going to be a genuine experience of how the Italian people live. I was ready. I was ecstatic!

There was another table in the living area which could seat six people. She had already set the table which included a setting for me.

I felt very welcome, and somewhat at home.

Dinner was very authentic and simple. Nothing elaborate, just a home-style Italian dinner. Pasta, in olive oil, some bread, and lots of homemade wine. Followed by cookies. Tina didn't bake much, but she always had packages of cookies and crackers on the table.

I was amazed at how the olive oil tasted. It was homemade, just three days old. It was like nothing I had ever tasted before. The flavor of the olives was so smooth.

Tina said the olive oil is lubrication in the veins like oil in a car. Not sure that's medically true, but we laughed.

She was so hospitable, and I felt very comfortable being there. We spoke a little about her and her farm and she said usually after dinner they have some grappa and play card games. Her husband Paolo was away for a couple of days'; but he was scheduled to return the next day.

After dinner Jonathan and I spoke for about an hour. Then I went to the cabin to unpack and he stayed and checked his emails. Wi-Fi was only available in the main cabin.

I rinsed-off in the small shower and lay in my bed reflecting on the activities of my day.

So much had happened in the course of just one day.

So many emotions.

Periods of extreme excitement, anxiety, fear and now peace.

Peace, knowing that I was where I was supposed to be this time in my life.

Peace, knowing that God brought me here to teach me something. To help me grow. I had so much to learn, and I was so very excited and at peace with my adventure!

In a foreign country with no knowledge of where I was, no knowledge of how to communicate. So alone, and yet feeling so embraced and cared for at the same time.

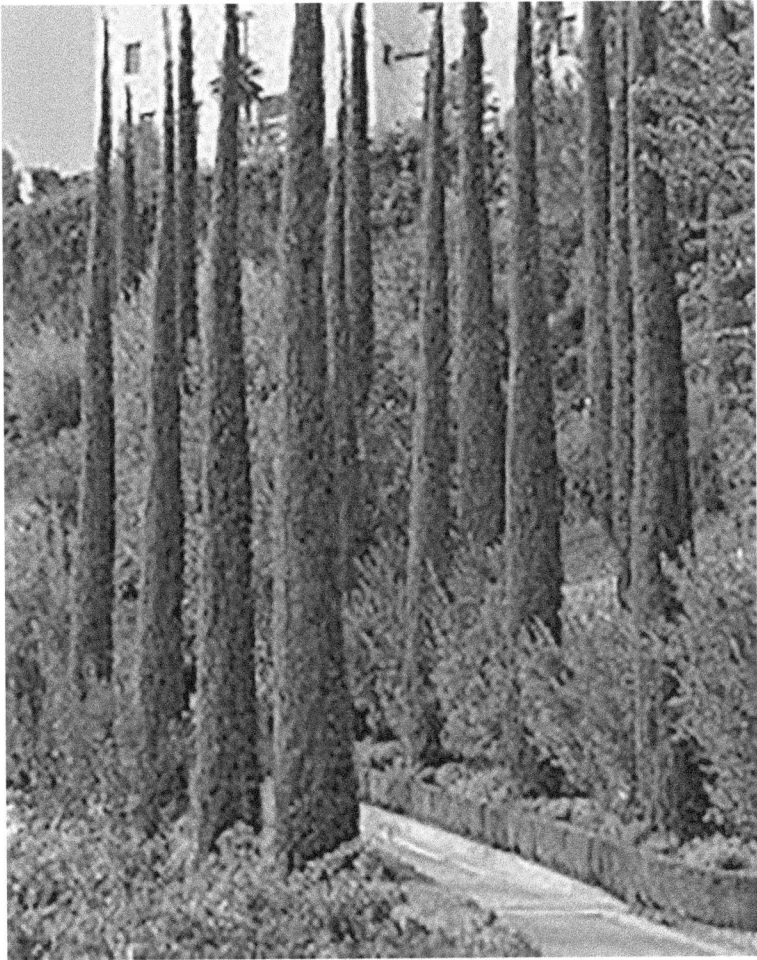

Italian Cypress trees

Chapter 6
Buona notte!

When I woke up the first morning in Italy, I opened the shutters of my bedroom window to check out the view.

There were mountains in the distance, but everything was hidden by a fog which seemed to camouflage the beauty I was expecting.

I went about settling in and when I looked over again at the window there was a cat sitting outside on the windowsill.

I later found out that this was one of Tina's eleven adopted outdoor cats. Strays who just seemed to settle at the farm. All of which were welcomed and fed by Tina. They were not allowed in the cabins, but they always tried to sneak in when the door was open.

After about an hour I walked out of my cabin to go to breakfast.

The fog had lifted. I looked across at the hills and valleys, while gazing upon the mountains. The air was fresh and crisp, and I just stopped and stared. I looked left, then right and I just couldn't get enough of it. The views were picturesque. There were farms, and roads, but the backdrop of the fields and the mountains was breath-taking.

I was overwhelmed with feelings of serenity. Ever so grateful to be in God's comforting hands. To experience the fullness of God's creation through the beauty of this place. These were the feelings that would welcome me for the next three weeks.

I could not believe I was here.

Here in Italy.

Living in Italy.

About to spend three weeks with an Italian family. Living like an Italian, not as an American in Italy.

I proceeded to the main house for the breakfast meal.

We had breakfast at eight thirty which I thought was late for farm workers.

Breakfast in Italy is pretty simple. A little toasted bread, some jam, Nutella which I later found seems to be a staple for any meal, some yogurt and cheese. First the espresso, or "long coffee" as Tina called American coffee. With breakfast, to my surprise we had tea with honey.

Tina joined us for breakfast which was a delight. After breakfast, Tina gave us our assignment.

There were some overgrown hedges which needed to be trimmed. I don't exaggerate when I say overgrown. These hedges were well over seven feet tall, and she wanted them trimmed to about five feet. WWOOFR rules stated that we were not allowed to use power tools, so she gave us some snippers and sent us on our way.

Just before we left, Tina remembered that the horses had not been fed, so she asked if we could do that before we began our work.

She had four horses. Beautiful as horses go. I'm not really a horse person, but these horses were fine looking animals. I just wanted to go over to them and pat their skin.

It was our job to toss some hay in their field to feed them. They were very happy to see us as we were to see them!

Trimming the hedges was difficult but not that physically demanding, and the weather was cool. The average temperature in this region of Tuscany in October is seventy-two degrees Fahrenheit. After a few hours of trimming we started getting hot. We had to step into the hedges in order to trim them, and I felt like I was in the African jungle sorting through the vines looking for Tarzan.

Jonathan and I enjoyed working together and the hours passed quickly. The age difference didn't appear as though it was going to be a problem. I was probably older than his Dad.

We finished, and Tina called us for lunch. She made pasta with olive oil, basil and garlic sauce, some focaccia, and fried battered fish croquettes.

As is customary with most meals there was a plate of fresh mozzarella. The kind of cheese that reminds you that you were really in Italy.

It was amazing.

A little bit about their water. Tina said you could drink it from the tap, but the town had a dispenser for local spring water, and it was available for people to fill their jugs for free. Tina said, "Water should be free." I laughed. Water in Italy comes in two varieties. Plain or with gas (naturally carbonated).

After lunch which ended at one-thirty, Tina said we were free to do whatever we wanted and we were to come back to work at three-thirty.

This was the "Italian Siesta", known in Italian as "Riposo." A traditional early afternoon shutdown which varies from business to business, but usually lasts from ninety minutes to two hours.

I went and sat outside and enjoyed the view.

I appreciated the fact that I was able to be there.

I enjoyed being an Italian in Italy.

We returned at three-thirty, and Tina took us to the hedges in the back that needed to be trimmed. That took us about an hour and a half to complete and she said, "okay see you at seven-thirty for dinner."

Before dinner I enjoyed a stroll across the farm in the night air. I was in awe of the city lights of Volterra, a nearby city, which lit up the sky atop a distant mountain.

It was magical.

The peaceful feeling of soaking up the views, breathing in the fresh crisp air, and knowing there was no place I would rather be.

I was astonished by the warmth of Tina's hospitality, and embracing the utter joy of this adventure.
I felt so blessed to be able to do this at this stage in my life.

To experience the beauty of such a place, and excited about what the future had in store for me, not only in the next coming weeks, but of the new journey in my life.

As I strolled down the road most of the eleven cats were strolling right behind me.

I could never feel alone in such a place as this.

John Wayne

Chapter 7
Grazie John Wayne and Paul Newman!

The next morning, I met Paolo, Tina's husband.

Paolo is on the timid side.

He is a strong, rugged looking man. Looked like a farmer. He was always dressed in an outfit that made him look like he was ready to go out and work the fields.

He didn't speak fluent English, but he always tried to teach us how to say things in Italian.

Tina would translate for us.

Paolo manages the labor part of running the farm, so we worked directly with him doing our daily chores.
Tina and Paolo's farm includes grape vineyards and olive trees.

I had done some research before I left for the trip on various methods of harvesting grapes and olives.

I was very excited, and very anxious about the process hoping I would be able to accomplish the tasks.

It turned out that the grape harvesting was completed the week before I arrived, and that we would only be harvesting the olives.

While we were eating breakfast with Tina, Paolo was at the groves examining the olive trees to see if we could pick the olives.

Over the last few days, it had been too muddy to pick the olives because they had experienced a lot of rain.

When Paolo returned, he said we could start picking in the afternoon but for now, more trimming.

Jonathan and I headed to the hedges and began trimming. We stopped for lunch at twelve-thirty, trimming completed.

Lunch was quite elaborate.

The usual staples, bread with olive oil, fresh buffalo mozzarella with basil. Tina served fresh pasta with olive oil and ricotta cheese, fresh pork sausage from the butcher on a nice salad with olive oil and Paolo's home-made balsamic vinegar.

We enjoyed some of Paolo's wine. Italian house rules: anytime is a good time for a glass of wine, or two.

Paolo is very proud of his wine, olive oil and vinegar, and he should be, they are all amazingly good.

After we ate, Paolo made espresso with a shot of grappa. Grappa is an alcoholic beverage: a fragrant, grape-based pomace brandy of Italian origin that contains 35 to 60 percent alcohol by volume (70 to 120 US proof). The flavor of grappa, like that of wine, depends on the type and quality of the grapes used, as well as the specifics of the distillation process.

Nice touch!

Our conversation led to how, for fun, Tina and Paolo would teach non-Italian speaking people how to say inappropriate things and bad words but not tell them they were bad words.

We laughed!

Paolo said they would tell young men how to flirt with Italian women but teach them bad things to say to the girls. All in fun of course and Tina said the girls would respond with a slap in the face.

Tina said they especially liked teaching her German guests' inappropriate phrases because her guests were a very proper people with a dry sense of humor. She said she would laugh when they spoke the phrases among other Italians. Her foreign guests looking confused as they were not aware of what Tina and Paolo were laughing about.

Tina and Paolo valued their friendships with all of their foreign guests and explained to them afterward what they had done, and how they were having fun with them. They would all laugh.

They shared with us how they enjoyed teaching some of their very proper Dutch guests' inappropriate words and watch them repeat them in a conversation very eloquently.

Paolo shared an interesting bit of Italian culture with us. He said his grandparents lived in the northernmost part of Italy, where the climate was similar to our climate in Alaska. They were poor, and the only heat source was a stove in the kitchen. He explained how everyone gathered in the kitchen to stay warm. They would all drink grappa to ward off the cold.

He said everyone had grappa, no matter what your age. Younger children would just get smaller portions.

This may be why, even in America, Italian gatherings usually end up in the kitchen. Paolo said the kitchen was the social gathering place for Italians.

Typically, Lunch break started around twelve-thirty. We would eat, talk, drink wine and then we were free to go off on our own, to enjoy our riposo, until three-thirty.

When we returned that day it started raining, so we worked with Tina.

She taught us how to make pasta, and a type of biscuit or doughnut called "Roschette". The biscuits were a concoction of flour olive oil and egg. I had a very hard time kneading the dough trying to make the little donuts, as she called them. Tina said it was a Jewish recipe.

Roschette are one of the typical products of Tuscan cuisine and in particular of the city of Livorno. The Livorno roschette are an ancient preparation rich in history in which the Italian culinary tradition is closely linked with Jewish history and culture. It was, in fact, the Sephardic Jews who were the first to bring the roschette to Livorno. Fleeing from persecutions suffered in the

Iberian Peninsula, the Jewish families arrived in the thriving seaport and here they were welcomed by the Leghorn families who, over the years, made their own recipe of Jewish kaaka, renaming them roschette and transforming them into one of the symbolic dishes of the city of Livorno.

Today roschette are one of the most famous dishes of the Livorno cuisine and are served as appetizers together with an appertif or to accompany cold main courses based on Tuscan cold cuts and cheeses.

Between narrow alleys and buildings where the old Jewish quarter was located, you may come across some old family-run bakery or restaurant where you can savor the ancient taste of roschette, or kaak, served with a strong black coffee as per tradition.

They resemble Italian tarallucci, or taralli, to some degree, but taste more like breadsticks. They are rings of dough made from flour, olive oil and water and they look like donuts, but they are not sweet at all.

We had them for dinner, and they were hard and dry. Not bad, just hard and dry. Not one of my favorite desserts.

We also had the pasta with a nice white sauce of butter and olive oil, for dinner. That, on the other hand was quite delicious.

Funny thing about Italian food in Italy versus Italian food in the U.S. We put red sauce on everything. They never use red sauce. At least not in this region of Italy.

Sauce was usually butter and truffles, which was always bursting with flavor and very good.

There is a big difference in the way Italians shop for food and groceries compared to most Americans. At least it is in this part of Italy.

For example, Tina buys fresh mozzarella and ricotta cheese from a local farmer. She buys fresh bread from the local bakery. She buys her meats from a local butcher every day or so.

This is a common practice because she appreciates the quality of fresh locally grown and produced products, and the importance of supporting local farmers and merchants.

Tina said when you are eating something of good quality you don't need to eat as much because you are completely satisfied. Whereas with inferior products you keep eating, searching for that satisfaction, and never achieving it.

That's such a good life lesson with people too. The importance and satisfaction of a meaningful relationship with friends and family versus superficial relationships with people.

That is the Italian way!

This is certainly true of Italian versus American eating habits. Italian meals contain much variety with small portions. Americans thrive on all you can eat buffets and large portions for meals.

We eat until it hurts sometimes.

Italians embrace their meals, they enjoy the quality of flavors and variety, and blend it together with wine, hospitality, and pleasant conversation.

After dinner we were talking about farming and raising animals and Jonathan asked about cattle. Jonathan was from Durango Colorado and cattle was a familiar subject for him.

Paolo's face lit up and he shouted "Cowboys!"

We laughed and they told us how in the sixties when they were children and TV was becoming popular in Italy, they all watched John Wayne movies. They always played "Cowboys and Indians," excuse the racial slur. Tina laughed at how the boys wore holsters and the girls, Indian headdress.

Who knew?

We laughed and talked about American movies in Italy.

The subject changed to parenting skills.

Paolo shared how he jokingly made his son and nephew gather stones from the garden to earn some money. They were only about ten years old. They would gather stones and Paolo would buy the stones back from the boys.

Then he taught them how to play poker and won all their money back from them.

He said he learned how to play Poker from a Paul Newman movie playing French Poker, which turns out to be similar to our five-card draw poker. He taught us, we played, drank wine, grappa and had a wonderful evening.

I was embracing our newly formed relationships.

I was learning so much about the simple, yet pure family life in Italy.

I was learning about the importance of relationships. How spending time talking, connecting, listening to others was so valuable. Time worth spending, sharing emotions hopes and dreams. Listening with an attentive ear and truly being interested in what other people are saying, and in between the lines, what they are actually going through.

The lack of emphasis on the things that had to be accomplished the next day, in comparison to sharing our hearts and lives.

Impacting others with our experiences and sharing different perspectives and ideals. It is truly a simpler way of life. Simple, yet complex.

I found myself bursting with emotions and feelings and it was fulfilling to the very core of my being.

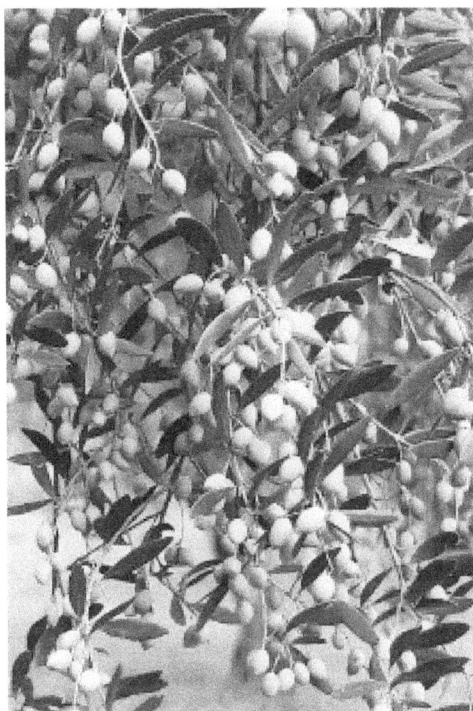

Olives on a tree

Chapter 8
Grazie a Dio!

Olive picking day had finally arrived.

Paolo told us to meet at nine a.m.

When we arrived at eight-fifty for breakfast, Tina was surprised that we were late.

We explained that Paolo told us nine. She proceeded to explain that was to start work, she said, "first you must eat breakfast."

Oops!

Paolo drove us to the olive groves in his little Land Rover-Defender. It was a small vehicle with benches in the rear. Jonathan and I jumped in the back. The groves were less than two kilometers down the street (La Strada).

We arrived to find various forms of large farm equipment housed in a huge garage structure.

We gathered our equipment to pick the olives. I don't know what I was expecting, but I thought there had to be some heavy-duty equipment and tools for us to use. Instead Jonathan handed me a small plastic claw-type hand rake. I said, "That's it?" Jonathan replied, "Yup!"

We grabbed six empty crates and loaded them onto a platform on the back of Paolo's tractor. Paolo packed his automatic picker, which was battery powered with an automotive battery. Jonathan and I stood on the platform of the tractor and off we went to the olive grove.

The path was muddy and bumpy, and at times I held on for dear life. Even though falling off the tractor would have only been a matter of a few inches to a soft muddy ground.

Picking olives is a pretty simple, yet effective process. We had to lay down netting, which extends to cover an area of about four or five trees. This is about fifty feet long by twenty feet wide. Then you just comb the branches with the hand claw and the olives fall to the ground on top of the netting.

Their olive trees were not very tall, so most of the branches could be handled with our hand claws. The trees are easy to climb because the trunk splits in the middle leaving a place to step and climb and reach the higher branches which were about seven feet high.

In some olive tree groves, where the trees are much older, the trees can get as high as twenty feet tall. On those farms you will see the pickers on step ladders, peeling off the olives.

Paolo's battery powered rake was simply two claws at the end of a stick that clapped in a very fast motion. Both the hand claws and the battery powered claws were very efficient.

The olives fell to the ground, and the branches were basically unharmed. After the olives had fallen to the ground, we would pick up the netting, gathering the olives and poured them into plastic crates.

Next, we would move the netting to the next group of trees and repeat the process. This was the strenuous part of our job. The net was heavy, and the grove was hilly, so dragging it up to the next section was difficult.

On the trees, the olives first appear green, and then they turn a shade of purple very similar to a grape depending on the ripeness. For our purposes all of the olives needed to be picked, and they were all blended in making the olive oil.

The work was not tedious, and it was actually quite fun, picking and chatting with Jonathan about life at home, and our families. We even spoke some religion and shared our beliefs.

We did this for about three hours. We picked about twenty trees and ended up with six crates full of olives. I later found out, that was our quota.

The weather was beautiful. Sunny, cool with a slight breeze, but after working for three hours I was drenched with sweat.

Paolo, a man of few words said, "Andiamo boys!"
It was time for lunch.

We jumped on the back of the tractor, headed back to the garage to unload the olives and equipment, got back in the Land Rover-Defender and we were off to the homestead.

Sweet!

Excited - about what surprises would be waiting on the table for our feast.

Grateful - and looking forward to a little rest and downtime.

There is nothing that works up an appetite better than a morning of olive picking. When we finished lunch, Tina said that Paolo wanted us back to work in a half hour.

Huh? I thought.

What happened to our afternoon siesta? I said to myself.

It was back to fields.

So many trees!

So much to pick!

I was starting to feel overwhelmed already!

We picked and picked, and Paolo was very focused. He would pick three trees to our one.

Jonathan and I split up, so we were all working independently.

Too much time to think.

I started thinking negative thoughts, "What have I gotten myself into?"

Jonathan was leaving Friday and next week it was just me . . . and Paolo!

I thought that there was no way I was going to be able to do this for another twelve days. Seven days with Paolo and then off to the other farm for five more days.

I have a lot of people rooting for me!

A lot of people counting on me!

A lot of people praying for me!

How could I ever face them and tell them I quit; I couldn't do that?

Ok, I decided I would do it for one more day, I would take it one day at a time.

Finally, Paolo shouted my name. I ran to him and he said, "Andiamo boys!"

Music to my ears!

I headed for the cabin for a nice shower and to sit in my chair and feel sorry for myself and weep!

I asked Jonathan if he wanted to shower first. He said no, he was going to go for a walk.

A walk?

Now I really felt old!

I limped back to my cabin and jumped in the shower. I actually crawled into the shower.

I put on my lounging clothes, my PJ's and sat in my chair. I thought to myself, well I may have said it out loud, how much I would love a beer. My exact words to myself were, "I would kill for a beer right now!"

When Jonathan came into the cabin. I asked him if he'd gone for his walk and he said he was about to.

He then asked me if I would like to go to town for a beer.

Because I had a car, and Jonathan did not I told him that anytime he would like to go to the local town to just let me know.

I couldn't get dressed fast enough, and we were on our way to town. The town Pontiginori, is about three blocks long, with a train station, bus stop, a grocery store, a bar, a tobacco store, a pharmacy and a church.

We chose the bar.

They had one beer on tap, San Miguel. We ordered a beer, and it was outstanding!

We had another.

We only had an hour break before dinner and the town was only ten minutes from the farm, so Jonathan and I sat at a table outside and life was good again!

Dinner with Tina and Paolo was delightful, as always. They wanted to retire early, so they said, "buona notte." We asked about tomorrow's agenda and Tina said Paolo had something to do so we were off until lunch tomorrow.

We asked Tina if there was a town we could visit in the morning, so she set us up for a road trip.

She said we would have to be back by one-thirty for lunch, but Jonathan and I thought it would be more fun if we had lunch out.

Tina said, "No problem, see you at two-thirty."

Working in the grove was challenging for me, a CPA whose heaviest piece of equipment is a stapler. Yet it was so gratifying, to see the fruits of our labor.

I never realized the effort it took to develop and strengthen trees to enable them to produce a good crop.

It was refreshing to see the pride Paolo took in his farm. How he yearned for a good harvest to produce an especially good batch of pure olive oil. It wasn't about profits, or wealth. The wealth was in the finished product. The satisfaction of working hard and seeing the fruits of your labor in the harvest.

I was humbled and delighted to know that I had a small part in this miracle.

San Gimignaino

Chapter 9
Che stupido!

The wooden shutters in my room refused to allow even a glimpse of light in.

Usually, when I opened the shutters the bright morning sky lit my room ablaze!

This morning I was excited about our half-day excursion. I tore open the shutters and to my dismay, no light came rushing in. The rain tapped on my window amidst the grey sky.

I assembled my clothing for my trip, which included my rain gear.

Jonathan and I were excited, nonetheless. We jumped into the car, set up the GPS and we were off and running.

Tina told us to visit San Gimignano, a small town about forty-five minutes away. That was the plan.

The drive took us over the mountain and down the other side. Narrow switch back roads up and down very steep slopes at times. Passing, and being passed by cyclists and local traffic. The Tuscan valleys did not disappoint. Even in the rain.

It took about an hour to get there, and the rain had subsided. I was concerned about parking as it is usually a problem anywhere you go in Italy. Lo and behold we found an actual parking lot!

I told Jonathan, "It is well worth the cost, whatever it was going to be!"

A short walk took us to the village gates.

A little history of San Gimignano.

San Gimignano mainly developed in the early Middle Ages, thanks to its favorable geographical position. Over time the Via Francigena became the route of pilgrims who traveled to Rome, mainly from France. The detour to the port of Pisa also went through San Gimignano, so that the town, by association with the Via Francigena, became one of the most important transit and stopping sites for all travelers.

San Gimignano dominates the top of a hill, clearly visible in the distance with its many tower houses. Today thirteen tower houses remain of the seventy-two tower homes of the fourteenth century, when every well-off family built a tower to show its economic power.

Almost all of the tower houses were built next to other buildings that were made of perishable materials such as wood and earth. In medieval times, the tower house was the higher symbol of power, mainly because the building process was not simple or cheap. Materials such as stone and marble needed to be excavated and transferred to town, and the building site arranged. Only the richest families of merchants and moneylenders could afford these works of construction.

The house occupied just part of the tower.

The ground floor consisted of workshops, the first floor of bedrooms, and the higher level of the kitchen. The kitchen, where a fire was usually lit, was located on the highest live-in room, to escape in case of accidental fire.

Unlike other towns such as Florence, Pisa, Lucca, and Siena, San Gimignano's architecture developed according to eclectic features, merging different styles and influences from different towns the Commune had come in contact with over time. The outcome is a very original and peculiar architecture.

As Jonathan and I entered through the city gates we stopped at a small cafe.

Jonathan wanted to blend in.

We didn't.

The bakery items were amazing, and they made several different types of crepes. I'm not usually a "crepe guy," but I thought, "What the heck?"

Breakfast was sweet, syrupy and delicious. The dining area was filled with shelves occupied by ornate bottles of liquor with glass sculptures in the bottles as well as a wide variety of wines.

We wandered through Piazza Pecori. On the side of the square there is the Lodge of Annunciation, also called the Lodge of the Baptistry, because of a hexagonal font which is beautifully engraved with scenes depicting the Baptism of Jesus.

We were amazed at all of the Piazza's.

The most beautiful square of the town was Piazza della Cisterna. In the middle there is an octagonal travertine well that gives the name to the square.

The most interesting structure was the Torre del Diavolo, the devil's tower.

The tower has a mysterious and unsettling name that is tied to a legend. It is said that upon returning from a trip, the owner noticed with great surprise that the tower was taller than when he left it. This miraculous event was immediately attributed to some diabolical intervention, and so the name of the tower became linked with the Devil.

Of all the piazza's and towers the most stunning beauty was the inside of the Duomo. The colors of the frescoes are so vivid and bright. We could have stayed for an hour and not been able to take it all in.

The village was full of energy and we enjoyed the open markets with vendors selling their goods.

Tina told us of a restaurant to eat at, and it was perfect. I even tried some pasta with wild boar, which tasted very similar to pulled pork.

Jonathan is a vegetarian, and he enjoyed some meatless pasta. The food was authentic and delicious. A glass of wine to complete our dining experience was the perfect touch.

We were able to walk along the perimeter of the second circle of the city walls. It was a very scenic walk with views of the surrounding hills of the Elsa valley.

As we departed, we fought with the parking lot machine. It was a totally automated process and after some struggle we successfully got out the gate. Parking was only eight Euro!

When we got back to the farm at two-fifteen (fourteen-fifteen) Paolo was standing at the door. He said, "Ready?" We ran into our cabin, changed into our work clothes and jumped into the vehicle with Paolo.

We picked for three hours.

Jonathan shared with me that he was a little overwhelmed the day before, as was I. He thought it was because we were not working side by side. No conversation and just a lot of time to think.

We worked side by side and the three hours went quickly and we were able to obtain our six-crate quota.

Jonathan asked Paolo if he wanted us to feed the horses and Paolo said, "Si'."

We went to the field together.

It was a one-man job, so I asked Jonathan if it was ok if I took my shower, and did he want to go for a beer afterward.

He thought that was a great idea.

As I was preparing for my shower Jonathan came in and said we were going to some restaurant with Tina in fifteen minutes.

Oh! Ok!

We showered, and got dressed for the occasion, not knowing what to expect.

We jumped into the car with Tina. Surprisingly, she didn't tell us anything about where we were going or why.

When we arrived at our destination, we were greeted by several people sitting around a table in a restaurant. Tina joined right in and Jonathan and I, well we felt and looked out of place. No one introduced us.

We sat down and observed.

One man seemed to be the leader because he started the discussion. Then he moved to another table filled with wine bottles and everybody gathered around that table. He started by opening a bottle and he asked whose wine it was.

All of the conversation was in Italian, of course.

He sniffed, shook the wine around, sniffed again, then he took a mouthful, swished it around in his mouth and spit it out.

We recognized this as a wine tasting technique. He appeared to be evaluating the wine, speaking to the person whose wine it was. He continued opening each of the bottles and giving rather extensive critiques of each of the wines.

Jonathan and I kept whispering to each other whether we thought he liked each wine or disliked it. The fact was it was not an approval or disapproval process, but more an instructional session for the wine makers.

The tasting ended and Tina gave us glasses and told us to taste whichever wines we liked.

She explained they were not fully developed wines yet. They were in the process of becoming wines. We nodded, but we didn't understand what that meant.

All the wines tasted terrible to us and Tina explained to us that this was how the wines tasted at this stage of processing. Then everyone sat at a large dining table and we were served food family style.

Everyone was so friendly and hospitable to us. Jonathan kept trying to speak Italian, and everyone laughed and enjoyed correcting him. He was charming and quite endearing to the women. They loved his attempts at the language and his boyish humility.

There were several different appetizers, and then the main course, pasta of course.

Everything was so tasty that I kept taking extra portions. It was at that point that I realized that being in Italy didn't make me Italian, because I ate like an American in Italy.

During dinner Tina explained that the man in charge was a "wine maker." He was an expert on wines, and he was advising the group of local wine producers how to adjust their wine to improve the final product.

No criticism, no rating the wines, just advise from the professional. What an unexpected delight. Tina explained how she wanted us to experience the entire process and that we could learn a lot about the wine making process by attending this tasting.

How thoughtful of her!

How unnecessary!

How appreciated by us!

To be among that insider group of local winemakers and getting a sense of the process they went through to produce a product of distinction was such a privilege.

Jonathan and I were simply hired labor to assist with the massive chore of harvesting olives and grapes.

Tina, however, did not view us in that manner. She wanted to share with us the intricacies of the process of making good wine.

Tina's desire was that we would understand how important it was to these local wine makers to produce the best wine they possibly could.

Not for money.

No one was going to get rich.

They took pride in the accomplishment of making a fine product of distinction.

The Mezzo Bridge

Chapter 10
Ero un po' deluso!

Tina had previously told us that she was participating in a food and wine festival in Pisa Friday through Sunday. The details were vague, but Jonathan and I were hoping to participate in some way.

At breakfast, Tina told us that she would like for us to go with her to the festival.

Jonathan and I were so excited. Not only to see the festival, but to be a part of it was beyond our wildest hopes and expectations.

She said we would have to pick olives in the morning with Paolo first, and go to the festival after lunch.

When we arrived at the grove, Paolo started walking toward the olive trees. This was odd because we usually would go by tractor. He was carrying three umbrellas and he motioned for us to follow him.

This was going to be another day of discovery.

We learned another method of picking.

You open the umbrella, invert it, and stick the point into the ground. Then you comb the olives from the branches with your fingers into the umbrella. When the umbrella became full, you dumped it into the crate.

Not very high tech, but very effective. Paolo said we did it this way because everything was too wet to pick in the traditional fashion.

We rather enjoyed that method. However, we only picked four crates compared to the prior picking sessions, where we usually filled six crates.

Jonathan and I were delighted to be going back for lunch and to get ready to go to the festival.

We showered and changed into nice clothes and had a quick lunch with Tina before heading to Pisa.

Pisa was about an hour drive and we arrived around four-thirty.

Pisa is a legendary city and one of the most famous in this region of Italy. It is one of the smaller cities in the Tuscany region, but has historically been one of the most important and influential.

From the eleventh century and onwards Pisa rose to prominence and became one of the major maritime republics of Italy. The city saw great development and it grew in population as investment was poured into the city to improve its infrastructure and build its world-famous monuments that still stand today.

Today, the city still maintains its ports, and this accounts for much of its economy, and it has a well-developed tourist infrastructure due to iconic buildings such as the Leaning Tower.

Pisa has an array of historic buildings and churches and beautiful scenery along the banks of the River Arno.

The River Arno is one of the main rivers in Italy, and Pisa was built around this waterway.

The section of the Arno that runs through Pisa provides a truly beautiful landscape and is an amazing place to simply walk along.

Five gorgeous bridges span the Arno in central Pisa.

The houses and the architecture create a gorgeous backdrop and the views are sublime.

The Mezzo bridge is one of the most beautiful and prominent bridges in Pisa that spans the River Arno.
The event that we attended was being held at a renovated train station, that was transformed into a convention center. When it was active, it was a hub for trains that ran from Pisa to Florence.

We found our display area and unpacked our wine and literature. We brought twelve cases of wine, which Jonathan and I unpacked and set up on the shelf unit behind our display table. Meanwhile Tina went to park the car.

Parking in Pisa is a nightmare, and thirty minutes passed until she finally returned.

We were able to walk around the event and view the other vendors. There were wine, olive oil, pastries, beer, fruits and yes, even a Gelato stand.

The festival and events were done very tastefully. Visitors could either sample everyone's products for free, or they could get a wine glass and purchase tickets to sample wines.

The local high school provided volunteer students to assist each vendor. Most of them were not helpful as they were distracted and just wanting to roam about the exhibit and play on their phones.

There was live music provided by a local jazz band who surprisingly played mostly familiar American songs. In English.

Go figure!

Tina bought us tickets for festivals' main event, the dinner, which turned out to be more of a presentation.

It was a pre-fix menu with three courses.

Before each course was served there were two chefs who displayed how they prepared the dish by actually preparing a dish live at the front of the dining area and projected it on a screen for all to see.

Each course was paired with a wine that was donated by one of the vendors. While they served the courses, the band played and a poet read some of his poetry, in Italian. It was done very nicely, but it took a bit too long in between courses. The meal lasted about two hours.

Throughout the festival Jonathan and I enjoyed standing at our display table pouring samples of Tina and Paolo's wine and conversing with some of the people that spoke English. Jonathan tried conversing in Italian to the people. To no avail, but they enjoyed his trying. I had given up trying. I had forgotten everything I learned about the language, and I was intent on just trying to understand what other people were saying. Quite honestly though, I was very disappointed that was not able to converse in Italian, let alone speak a fluid sentence.

Seeing all the couples, and families, and some people with their dogs made me homesick.

The event was to be held Friday, Saturday, and Sunday. When Tina first asked us to help her with the festival, I explained to her that I had planned on visiting the nearby town of Volterra on the weekend. She said I should go on my excursion on Saturday because Jonathan was helping her and asked if I could help her Sunday.

What could I say? Of course, I would!

WWOOFR's are not supposed to work on the weekends. I was happy to oblige, as I considered this more of a privilege than part of our job.

Saturday was going to be Jonathan's last day with Tina. He was going to be working on another farm in the area for the next three weeks.

He had been with Tina two weeks.

Tina and Paolo loved having Jonathan and told him not to go to the other farm, but Jonathan had already committed to working there.

I thought, "it's going to be weird for me to be the only one there with Tina and Paolo next week."

I wished he was staying too.

Jonathan and I were from two different worlds. He was a student coming of age and I had already experienced most of life's events, getting married, raising a family and developing a career.

He was from the Colorado Rockies, and I was from New Jersey and New York, the big cities in the Northeast.

We developed such a kinship which was beyond logic given our circumstances.

Soon we would be going back home to our lives. Our journey would come to an end, and we would take with us valuable lessons learned from our experiences together. Each of us learning different things, experiencing different feelings and emotions.

We were two totally different people, in very different stages of our lives, yet for a time we had been joined together to share a very important time in our lives.

God brought us together, to share this part of our lives. To help us to learn, grow, and for me, to heal.

Volterra

Chapter 11
Arrivederci Amico mio!

Volterra!

That was my next destination scheduled for Saturday, and Jonathan was off to his next adventure on a different farm.

We left at the same time, so I had a chance to say, "Arriverderce" to my new Amico!

I set the GPS for Volterra and off I went.

Volterra was the last of the Etruscan cities to be conquered by the Romans. It sits atop the mountain and was well fortified, which was why the Romans had such a difficult time conquering the city.

The Etruscans were one of the people that inhabited parts of Italy in ancient times before the Romans took over the peninsula.

It was an important Etruscan center, one of the "twelve cities" of the Etruscan League.

The city offers a rich array of ruins, art works and architecture from different historical periods. Its pristine streets and spacious squares make it a favored Tuscan hill town.

It took me half an hour circling the city to finally find the correct parking lot, which was underground, but right at the city gate.

Jonathan had visited Volterra and he said he got lost several times walking around the city even with his map.

I was a little anxious about not being able to find my car. I took a picture of my license plate, and the parking garage sign which told me I was parked on the second piano, second level down. Luckily, I was parked right by the elevator which took me right to the exit, which was just a few steps from the entrance to the city.

Jonathan told me he spent six hours touring the city and didn't get to see everything.

Cautiously, I entered the city.

The crowds flowed to the main piazza, so I followed, noticing every landmark so I would know where I was. I saw a sign for the information office, so I went in and grabbed a map and inquired as to which were the main sites to see. The clerk pointed out some highlights on the map and sent me on my way. Luckily, she spoke fluent English. The city was not that complicated to me, so I was relieved.

I stopped for coffee at the first crowded restaurant. I enjoyed an American coffee and a cream filled Danish. All Italian coffee is espresso, American coffee was simply espresso with extra hot water and cream.

I was happy to be off to a very good start.

After my coffee I checked the time. It was ten AM. I mapped my route and took off. I'm not much of a "museum buff" so I figured I would be finished viewing the artifacts in the museum in rapid time.

I strolled very slowly, looking at every shop.

My first stop was the Etruscan museum. I was intrigued by the Etruscan history - what little is known of it.

The museum was bursting with ancient artifacts. Stone sculptures, bronze, metal and gold pieces. But after you've seen one or two, you're good.

At least I am.

I raced through the three floors of ancient artifacts and I was on my way.

I enjoyed the various parts of the city. Of course, there were churches and a cathedral. I visited the churches, marveling at the art and mosaics inside but I tend to glance, admire, and move on rather rapidly.

The place where I did spend a lot of time admiring was the piazza with the food trucks.

Of course!

Lots of fruits and vegetables, food trucks selling fine cheeses and meats. There was even a food truck selling fresh fish.

I sampled some pork and cheese and moved along.

Once again, I was struggling with being there alone. I missed not having my wife with me.

Part of the joy of seeing new things, and discovering new experiences is having someone to share them with. My wife and I shared so many great experiences and places while we were together that it hurt not to have her with me to share this place.

I continued to pray all morning and the ache went away.

I hit all the hot spots, and even the not so hot spots and it was only eleven forty-five. I set a goal to stop for pizza at twelve, so I toured the streets for a good crowded pizza place.

While I was touring, I found a rather large wine store. I wanted to get Tina and Paolo a gift for their kindness and hospitality when I left, so I went in.

Knowing that Paolo was a wine maker, I knew buying wine for him was going to be a very difficult task.

I asked the saleswoman what was her best wine from Volterra? She didn't speak much English, but I tried to explain that it was a gift for someone who also makes wine. She brought me three bottles. One of them was one hundred percent Sangiovese which is what Paolo makes, and it was made in Volterra, and it was the most expensive bottle she had.

I bought it.

I decided on a restaurant and by now it was past twelve, so I was good to go for my pizza escapade.

Nice place, nice pizza. A success story!

Now it was one o'clock and I had already toured the entire city one and a half times.

There was nothing to go home to, so I strolled through the archeological park on the other side of the city. It was peaceful and serene, and it killed an hour.

Ok I was done!

I found my car without any problem, and I even remembered how to pay for the parking.

I got into my car, set the GPS and I was off.

I opened the windows of my car, plugged in my iPhone and put the volume way up.

Cruising through the hills of Tuscany I felt very happy, confident, and content to be in Italy just driving through the countryside on a beautiful sunny yet cool day listening to American music. It was classic rock, so I was in my glory with the car windows down blasting some classic Led Zeppelin songs.

I got back to the farm around two forty-five and Jonathan had not left yet. It turned out that he was not able to go to the festival, instead he was picking olives all morning with Paolo. I felt as if I had deserted them.

We chatted about Volterra a little and we said our good-bye's once again.

We had only been together for a week, but Jonathan and I had developed such a good friendship and I was sad for us to part.

We had enjoyed working hard side by side. We had good discussions during our times in the field.

Our little getaway bar became our "go to" spot after a hard day's work just before each dinner.

He was a very sociable, likeable boy, and people gravitated to him at the bar. He was not legal age in the U.S., but he was in Italy, so he loved graduating to that level, being able to drink and hang out at the bar.

His Italian was terrible, but all the locals loved how he tried, and loved to talk to him and instruct him on the language.

I was going to miss him!

Roman Olive Press

Chapter 12
Benvenuti a casa, Jonathan!

My first night without my buddy Jonathan was very rough.
I returned from dinner to an empty cabin.

I was feeling so alone.

I was feeling more anxious now than when I first arrived. Having had a buddy to share this experience with, I was now feeling the loss.

I laid down to sleep and I just couldn't shake the feeling of being alone. I plugged in my ear buds and fell asleep to the comforting sounds of my music.

I woke up and checked the time. It was only one-thirty.

I laid there listening to my music thinking . . . thinking . . . thinking! I glanced at my phone to check the time. It was now three-fifteen in the morning. Ugh!
Finally, I fell asleep shortly thereafter.

I was told to come for breakfast at eight-thirty, where we would come up with a game plan for the day. I strolled over at eight-thirty and the doors to the living area were still locked.

Paolo's car was not in the driveway, but Tina's was. I went to my cabin, got my book and figured I would just wait in the lobby area until she arrived.

She showed up at nine-thirty.

She apologized for being late, but told me that the festival didn't end until after eleven-thirty the night before and by the time she got home it was after one AM.

She had worked at the festival for over twelve hours and was exhausted.

I told her not to worry about preparing anything for breakfast, so she put out some biscuits (Cookies) and made some tea and coffee.

Tina asked if I would come to the festival again, in case there were some English-speaking people that did not speak Italian.

This was totally unnecessary because she speaks and understands English quite well, but I was happy to oblige.

She said to come back at eleven, and we would leave. I offered to help her with some kitchen chores, so she agreed to let me come back at ten-thirty to dry the dishes.

We agreed that I would drive separately in my car because the festival would not end till eleven-thirty that evening, and she did not want me to have to stay so late.

My GPS did not recognize the restored train station in Pisa, so Tina picked the new train station as my destination. Since I was following her that seemed appropriate.

The snag was when we went on the motorway, as they call the toll highway. That's right, it was a toll road. The problem was that Tina had an automated toll sticker and I did not. I drove through the manual toll booth and picked up a ticket and she was waiting in the right-hand lane for me when I exited the toll booth.

The toll is based upon how far you travel on the highway. When you enter the motorway, you pick up a ticket, and when you exit, it calculates how much you owe by the distance you have travelled.

At the exit I handed the toll taker my ticket. She told me how much it was, and I shuffled through my pockets to pay her. When I left the toll booth Tina was nowhere to be found!

I carefully followed my GPS and it took me right to my destination.

The wrong one.

It took me to the new train station.

I wrote down the correct location, but my GPS would not recognize it no matter how I tried to put it in.

I stopped my car in back of a parked car and walked up to the fellow in the car. I asked if he spoke English and his answer, which was the typical answer I was getting from people when asked that question was, "Parlo un po 'di inglese." I asked him where the correct train station was, and he told me to go to the light make a right and it's a few streets down on the right.

Really?

He was right.

Now to find a parking space.

I drove around the station and someone was pulling out right near the entrance.

Sweet!

As I was parking, I saw Tina walking right by my car. I called to her and we were both so happy that I made it!

As we were walking to our booth, she told me Jonathan was coming back.

"What?", I screamed!

She said Paolo was going to pick him up later that afternoon.

The festival was a delight. Watching the people as they strolled by our display table was such a treat! Tina had sold a lot of wine and I was very happy about that.

I was observing the people that stopped at our table. They would converse with Tina, and it seemed that everybody just loved to talk. They would sip the wine and chat with Tina. I had no idea what they were saying but they really seemed to enjoy talking with each other.

At about five-thirty I asked Tina if I could leave and she said that would be fine. She told me that Paolo had picked up Jonathan.

I texted Jonathan and asked if he would like to go for pizza when I returned, and he said yes.

It took about an hour to get home.

I was feeling pretty confident navigating the roads now.

When I arrived, Jonathan was watching a DVD in Tina's living room, which was a common area for guests.

We were happy to see each other, and we resorted to hugs.

Jonathan was very uncomfortable with the new farm owners where he was supposed to work at. He said they were not native Italians and although they spoke fluent Italian, they did not want Jonathan to speak any Italian.

A side note about Jonathan here. He's a Colorado boy who wanted to blend in with the Italians. Light hair, blue eyes, light complexion. He was always talking about how he stands out as not being Italian. In fact, he asked Tina what he could do to look more Italian. Jonathan loved learning Italian and was always asking Tina and Paolo how to say things. His favorite word was

"Fantastico!"

When the new farm owners told him not to speak Italian he was devastated.

The new farmers had a dry, or no sense of humor so Jonathan struggled with that too.

The straw that broke the camels' back was that they had no olives to pick.

Jonathan was scheduled to stay at that farm for three weeks. They said they would find things for him to do around the house.

Tina and Paolo gave him an open invitation to come back when he left. They even tried to talk him into not going. He called Tina and asked if he could come back.

When Tina told me why Jonathan was coming back my mind started racing with fear and anxiety again about my next farm.

What if the farm I was going to next week was a really bad place?

What if the accommodations were terrible?

What if I was stuck sharing a bedroom with three or four other strangers?

Should I stick with what I know?

Should I ask Tina if I could stay an extra week?

After all, I got along well with Tina and Paolo, and I now had Jonathan, and the living conditions were great!

But what about my sense of adventure?

Was I taking the cowardly route?

Think . . . Think . . . Think!

Jonathan and I had a great dinner. Our discussion during dinner revolved around my thoughts about next week. He had plans to go to another farm the following week, and shared that he had the same feelings and concerns that I had about leaving.

I thought, "Maybe we could both stay at Tina's."

"Maybe we could both go to my next farm together."

I thought, going as a team would make it a lot easier to bear if the conditions were bad.

It was such a warm feeling to have made such a friendship with Jonathan.

I had a lot of thinking to do. I had to make a decision, and there were so many factors affecting that decision.

Adventure or comfort?

I was shying away from the adventurous aspect in favor of a more pleasant, safer environment in which I knew what I had.

Maybe I'm just too old for this kind of adventure, I thought.

Yet, look at all that has come of my overcoming my fear and anxiety and taking this adventure in the first place.

Oh my, "God help me" I prayed!

Siena

Chapter 13
Mamma Mia!

The next two days were business as usual.

After breakfast we would pick olives for a few hours, return for lunch and after lunch we would pick for a few more hours.

We were getting into a routine and the time passed quickly. By the end of the picking session each day we were both very tired.

It wasn't the picking that was tedious, it was picking up the net and dragging it to the next location that was very strenuous. It was a very large and heavy netting and dragging it up the hills of the grove was exhausting.

The two days that Jonathan was gone I discovered a local restaurant that made great pizza. I also visited the small grocery store in Ponteginori the small town about five minutes from our farm.

After our picking session, before dinner was ready, we went to the grocery store. He was so excited. I think he bought every cookie they had!

Jonathan was smitten, by the grocery store clerk. She was an attractive young woman, and he tried flirting with her in his semi-Italian way. She was receptive and over the next few days, he kept asking me how to invite her to go for a drink at the bar.

He eventually asked her, but they never found a mutual time to meet.

We visited the tobacco shop in Ponteginori and bought a few different types of small cigars. We then wandered over to the bar had a few beers, and smoked our cigars. I could sense Jonathan enjoying his newly found coming of age ability to sip a beer and smoke freely.

Jonathan started getting anxious about his plans.

The next two weeks he was supposed to be at that other farm where he only lasted two days. He wanted to stay with Tina and Paolo another week, but he did not want to ask, as he felt he was imposing. I felt confident that they would enjoy having him stay there a little longer, and I assured him that they would appreciate his help for another week.

He started looking for other farms on the internet, and he was going to start calling and emailing them to see if they could accommodate him.

I contacted the farm I was scheduled to go to and asked if Jonathan could come along. The farm owner responded that he did not have room for Jonathan.

Meanwhile, I was thinking, I've experienced the olive picking and life on a farm, maybe I should cancel my next week and become a tourist. After all, I was in Italy!

Maybe this second farm would be a totally different experience.

Should I really give that up?

Where was my sense of adventure?

Anxiety was building, and Jonathan said, after dinner he was going to do some serious research on his tablet.

I started looking for hotels in Siena and Florence.

Tina made a wonderful lasagna for dinner. Traditional Italian lasagna without red sauce. It was delicious!
I decided to give Tina and Paolo the wine I bought for them in Volterra.

She said Paolo was so tired that he laid down on the bed and did not want to be disturbed for dinner. I guess we wore him out! Unlikely!

Tina was so excited about the wine. She said she knew the winemakers, and this was a new wine that they wanted to try.

Dinner was great and we enjoyed the wine.

During dinner, the conversation turned to a discussion with Jonathan. Tina asked if he was staying another week with them, and he asked if they could use his help. She assured him that he was welcome, and they would love for him to stay.

He was ecstatic!

Then Tina turned to me and asked about my plans.

She knew about my other farm and asked if I would like to stay with them for another week.

I said I would like that very much!

Jonathan and I were very happy with that plan.
Decisions made! We would stay and work for another week.

Saturday, we decided to visit Siena as tourists, and the following Saturday possibly Jonathan would visit Florence with me as a tourist on his way to another farm.
Sounded like a good plan. We went to bed relieved.

As I was lying in bed making notes on my laptop, I heard a fly buzzing around my bedroom. I stopped and tried to follow the buzzing but then it stopped.

I continued on my laptop and there it was again. This time I got up and followed the fly around the room, and then I lost it again. This went on for about an hour jumping out of bed every five minutes to try to swat that fly.

Every time I settled back in bed with my computer, buzz . . . buzz . . . buzz!

Finally, he landed beside my nightstand and I put an end to him!

I spent some time praying, realizing that faith is trusting in what we cannot see, what we do not know. Trusting that God is in control, and even when we cannot see the plan, God has one, and He is always in control.

Palio di Siena

Chapter 14
Fantastico!

When we woke up, we didn't know how to dress. Our plans were uncertain whether we would be working on the farm or doing something different. There was a major communication breakdown.

Jonathan and I held a meeting in our cabin, and we decided to get dressed for work.

The situation was this: Paolo said we would work in the morning and not in the afternoon because he had to go to Pisa in the afternoon.

Tina said we would be off in the morning and work in the afternoon because Paolo had to go to Pisa in the morning.

When we arrived at breakfast Tina informed us that we would be working Friday and Saturday and we could have the day off.

One thing Jonathan and I had come to expect of Tina and Paolo is to always expect the unexpected!

In the meantime, Tina was making plans for us to sightsee with her on Sunday.

I was a little disappointed that Tina wanted us to work Saturday. I had planned to visit Siena on Saturday.

I told Tina I had hoped to go to Siena Saturday, and she said it would be wonderful to go today.

Uh! Okay!

Jonathan and I took off for Siena.

When we arrived in Sienna, we started at the Piazza del Campo which is the heart of Siena. It's a huge square and is considered one of Europe's greatest medieval squares.

We took time to enjoy a cup of coffee in one of the bars there.

The Duomo of Siena is impossible to miss. It is a Gothic building filled with many treasures.

The Torre del Mangia inside the Public Palace in Piazza del Campo is quite a specimen of architecture.

To reach the top of the tower you have to climb four hundred steps, and the views of the town and surrounding countryside are simply terrific.

Jonathan had to go to the top.

I gladly went back to the bar for another coffee.

The main event that takes place in Siena is the Palio. The Palio is a horse race which takes place two times a year and is run in the Piazza del Campo, which is transformed for the occasion into a sand field.

We had a great day admiring the architecture and enjoyed observing the people of Siena!

For lunch we found a fast-food pasta store. You pick your pasta, pick your sauce. They mix it all together in a disposable bowl and off you go!

What a concept. We enjoyed that much more than a greasy burger and French fries. Finally, I got to have my pasta with "red sauce."

As we strolled through the streets, we stopped at a bakery and bought some Italian cookies for Tina . . . and for us.

We headed home. Dinner was at eight.

The dinner conversation led to questions about the U.S.

Tina was curious about how things were developing in the U.S. today, and Paolo wished that the America that he learned about as a child still remained as it was.

As I said before, their childhood images of America came from American western films.

Tina shared that they learned a lot about American customs and traditions through Charlie Brown comics and cartoons.

She said they also learned a lot from watching Donald Ducks' uncle Ludwig Von Drake, through his educational cartoons.

Go Figure!

Paolo told us that his son was studying cinema and art history at the university in Rome. He said his son was doing set design for films and Paolo was very excited about that.

Paolo said one of his favorite movies was, "Gangs of New York." He remarked at how the set design was one of the things that made the movie great. He had the movie in his video library, and we watched it after dinner. I was reminded of my grandparents' plight, coming to America.

Jonathan and I had bought some microwave popcorn at the market and we taught Tina how to make popcorn in the microwave. She rarely, if ever, used the microwave.

I was amazed how our American ways and traditions were observed and viewed, even idolized by people outside the United States.

As an American I am very naïve of foreign countries and people. Of how they live, and how they view the U.S.

That night I learned so much about influence.

111

I learned how film makers in Hollywood could impact the entire world. I realized how much power they had, to represent and portray our societies' traditions, even our morals and beliefs in a film to the world.

I learned that how we live our life, affects the people we come in contact with.

We represent our culture, and our heritage to others. Something we often take too lightly.

I realized that how I behaved here in Italy on this journey, would be a representation to Tina and Paolo of who American people are, and what we believe and stand for.

It made me think! I was the ambassador for my country, and God.

I was not worthy of such an honor and assignment, but God often chooses ordinary people to accomplish His work.

Olives in netting after harvesting

Chapter 15
Era una giornata indaffarata!

When I woke up and opened my window shutters, one of Tina's cats was sitting on my windowsill looking in.

A little bit about the cats. All eleven cats were always lingering around the front door looking for an opportunity to dash into the house.

They were friendly and affectionate, and they would follow us wherever we walked.

I am not really much of a "cat-person," but something about these cats was alluring.

One day I decided to take a walk down the road, and when I looked back five of the cats were following behind me.

The cat on the windowsill was grey and had only three legs. She had lost a leg in a hunting accident, but she ran around just like the other cats.

They called her "Tripod."

The morning was filled with frequent gunshots from the local hunters which was pretty normal for this time of year. They hunted mostly for rabbit and wild boar.

I dressed for work and I went outside to wait for Jonathan to go to breakfast.

It was another amazing day. The sun was shining, the air was crisp, and it was beautifully cool. I stopped and gazed at the mountains and the valleys and thought how blessed I was to be here.

After breakfast, we headed off to the olive grove.

As I was picking the olives a feeling of calmness and contentment swept over me.

I felt I was exactly where I was supposed to be right now.

It wasn't about the work. It didn't matter if I picked one olive, or a thousand. It was a time of respite. A time to learn, a time to grow. God had placed me here, in this place to rest. To take time to absorb his creation. To experience the beauty of the earth and the stars.

The beauty of relationships between people.

A time of healing.

I felt His peace.

Lunch was amazing, home-made ravioli. I kept forgetting that their lunch meal was a main meal, and not just a light sandwich.

During lunch Tina explained that there was a change of plans.

This came as no surprise!

She had to bring some wine to a local restaurant in Pisa. She was trying to convince him to buy her wine for his customers.

Her plan was to include us, and she would take us on a route through her hometown, Livorno.

Livorno is a port city on the western coast of Tuscany, on the Ligurian Sea.

They simply refer to it as, "The Sea."

After that, she said we would head to Pisa where we could go to the supermarket to get some groceries.

I was delighted that Tina included us in her chores, and that she wanted to teach us and show us all aspects of her life.

I was tired from a rather long session of picking olives, but I thought, "What the heck?"

It was a bright and sunny Saturday afternoon, and the road was alongside the coast, so we had a very beautiful view of "The Sea."

It was very crowded and there were cars and scooters parked everywhere along the road. Tina parked at a bus stop. She said we would only be a few minutes, so it was ok.

We walked to the water and it was bursting with people sitting on the rocks that were jutting into the sea.

She showed us her little boat that she had docked there in a little marina. It was a small boat, a little larger than a rowboat with a little engine. Unfortunately, they rarely had time to go out and enjoy it.

We went back to the car and drove a little further and stopped again.

She parked in another bus stop and we visited a bar. It was jumping, people were everywhere enjoying the weekend.

Tina wanted to introduce us to a "Spritz." In Italy this is considered an aperitif or aperitivo - a refreshing, before dinner cocktail. It's a simple mixture of either Campari or Aperol (Campari is less sweet and more bitter than Aperol, which is preferred), club soda, prosecco, ice and an orange slice. We stood by a table outside and enjoyed our cocktail as there were no seats to be found.

The coast in Livorno reminded me of our beach towns along the Jersey shore.

Off to Pisa.

When we arrived at the restaurant, we brought in two bottles of Tina's wine and sat with the restaurant owner. He was a younger man, around thirty-five. He spoke very little English but occasionally, during their conversation he would look to Jonathan and me and say something in English.

He opened a bottle of wine and we had a glass during our meeting.

Tina said the meeting went well. We took her word for it, and we took off for the supermarket.

When we arrived at the supermarket I thought, "Welcome to the U.S."

This was a "superstore." It was a combination department store / supermarket. It was crowded, and vibrant. Tina was overwhelmed entering and she laughed saying, "Okay, let's experience this."

This was not a new adventure for me, because this was the type of market that I was accustomed to back home.

It appeared that the Italian people have taken to the modern way of shopping. At least here in Pisa.

I laughed when I heard the Asian chefs preparing sushi speaking Italian.

Tina found everything she was looking for in the way of groceries and we were on our way.

Tina said the store was, "wild and crazy," but I think there was a part of her that liked it.

As she was walking through the grocery section, I saw her eyes light up as she saw the wide variety of items available all in one place. I think Tina could get used to this place. The first step in the modernization of Tina, maybe!

It was eight o'clock and there was still an hour drive to get home. This would be a late dinner, even by Italian standards so Tina asked if we would like to pick up some pizza and bring it home for dinner.

When we arrived at the pizza place near the farm it was almost nine thirty and Tina asked if we would prefer to eat there. I agreed, that was a better idea. We pulled into the restaurant parking lot and it was absolutely full. We decided not to stay.

We drove down to our local bar in Ponteginori and decided to have a drink and a snack.

When we got back to the farm Tina said she would make some pasta. It was now well after ten. We told her it wasn't necessary, but she insisted. So, she made some pasta and we ate while watching a movie.

It was a very long and exhausting, yet fulfilling day.

I was very tired but watching the movie and eating the pasta just felt right.

We were one big happy family. Traveling together, so comfortable with each other. It was if we had known each other our entire lives.

Cecina, Italy

Chapter 16
Sogni d'oro!

It was Sunday, our day off!

It was hard for me to fathom that I was in Italy, on a beautiful morning with the freedom to travel and do whatever I desired. In Italy. What a delightful feeling. We decided to drive to Cecina for breakfast.

Cecina was a little city about thirty kilometers from the farm. Jonathan had been there, I had not.

I decided that I should get a souvenir for my grandchildren. I thought I would get some T-shirts, but Jonathan said his grandpa used to buy him socks whenever he traveled. He told me how memorable that was for him. Fond memories of his grandpa's travels. That sounded like a good idea, so off we went. The quest for "socks."

Cecina was a delightful little city. We found parking in the Centro, walked up a few streets and stumbled upon a street flea market. We worked our way through the vendors' displays looking for a place to have breakfast.

We were both in the mood for a good American-style sit down breakfast. Pancakes, eggs and potatoes for a start.

There was no such thing.

At least not in Cecina.

We settled in at a wonderful cafe and had our traditional carb-loaded breakfast of croissants and coffee.

We then proceeded to view the vendors selling their wares.

The majority of the tables were filled with used vintage household items from people's homes. It was interesting and fun to see the variety of goods available. Particularly how the household items in Italy were so different than what you would find in the U.S.

We were so excited when we came across a Charlie Brown vintage collection of old comics, hard bound in a book. The vendor wanted five Euro. We said, "too much," and we offered him three. He said no, it was a collectors' item. Being shrewd negotiators, we gave him the five Euro. We thought it would be a good gift for Tina.

As we continued our shopping spree, we saw a book of Mickey Mouse Western comics.

Cowboys! We immediately thought of Paolo.

It was a different vendor and he said he wanted two Euro. We bought it without a fight, as a gift for Paolo.

Further down the street we saw a collection of cowboy comic books called "Tex." These were only one Euro each. We thought this would be an even better gift for Paolo. We perused the collection in search for a comic about, "Cowboys and Indians" as they were referred to back in the day.

Sidebar: Jonathan is originally from Durango and Paolo kept saying how he wanted to visit Durango and see the cowboys in a saloon.

We found a comic which featured a character called "Tex." It was entitled, "The sheriff of Durango."

We scoffed it up!

After the street fair, we decided to visit, "the Sea" in Cecina.

We found parking, which was, as usual, a difficult task and we proceeded to walk toward the beach.

The beach consisted of soft black and grey stone and volcanic sand. Unlike the beaches on the Jersey shore which were pure sand.

Being from Colorado, Jonathan was not accustomed to the beach.

Needless to say, he was super excited. Taking off his shoes he put his feet in the water. He said the water was really warm.

It was a beautiful sunny day, around seventy degrees. No one was in the water but there were people laying in the sand and sitting on the rock jetty's enjoying the sun.

Jonathan kept saying how he wanted to go for a swim.

The next thing I knew he was stripping down to his shorts and heading for the water.

No one seemed to mind.

He was so happy.

After his little swim, we walked to a little bar on the beach. Jonathan, in his boxers carrying his clothes. He sat down, and we enjoyed a couple of beers waiting for his clothes to dry.

He got dressed and we walked along the beach.

We went down the street that was parallel to the beach because there was a street festival of food vendors grilling and selling their food from trucks and stands.

The air was bursting with aromas of flavors and spices. We sampled some street food: Sausage & Peppers, Meatballs, Meats on a stick, Pastas and more. Desserts included Zeppole, sometimes called fritelle, which is an Italian pastry consisting of a deep-fried dough ball of varying size but typically about four inches in diameter. There was an abundance of Cannoli, which means "little tube" This is also an Italian pastry that originated on the island of Sicily. They are tube-shaped shells of fried pastry dough, filled with a sweet, creamy filling usually containing ricotta. Cookies of all varieties and of course lots of Gelato.

The swimming area of the beach ended, but the beach itself continued into a forest of pine trees.

They were not the typical pine trees that you would find in New Jersey. These trees, called "stone pines" had regular tree barks and had bright green leaves starting about thirty feet high. These are the pine trees that produce pine nuts, known in Italian as "Pignoli" nuts. They are very popular in the making of holiday cookies.

Walking back to the car we went down a different street which was lined with the pine trees.

It was a pretty sight for sure.

We returned home around three o'clock and noticed the time on the car radio was off by an hour. We were puzzled, until we realized later that Italy turned their clocks back for daylight savings time a week earlier than the U.S.

When we got back to the farm, we met Tina who informed us that she wanted us to help her make some Gnocchi Romana, which was Gnocchi made from Semolina flour at seven o'clock.

We went back to our cabin and I sat outside reading for a little bit. After which Jonathan and I went into town to have a drink.

We returned at seven o'clock ready for our gnocchi adventure.

Tina actually opened a cookbook and said, "first we will make crepes." But as she was turning the pages, the page after the crepes was a recipe for pancakes. Well, since we didn't get our American breakfast in Cecina, which would have included pancakes, that page caught my eye.

I shared that with Tina, and she said they don't typically make pancakes, but it would be fine for us to make them for dinner. I thought of explaining that they would be better in the morning, but I didn't bother.

She was putting the ingredients together in her mixer. As she was doing it, I noticed she put in a huge amount of sugar. I thought that was odd, but what did I know. When she gave me the batter to start cooking the pancakes, I noticed the batter was very watery. I told her something was wrong, she told me to add more flour. We kept adding flour and it got a little better, but then we ran out of flour. Jonathan said he thought it would be OK.

It wasn't.

The batter was so runny that the pancakes ran all over the frying pan and cooked very thin, like crepes.

After a few pancakes, I re-read the recipe. It called for 20kg of sugar and 200kg of flour. Tina put in 20kg of flour and 200kg of sugar.

When I told Tina we all laughed.

They tasted good, but they were not pancakes. They certainly were very sweet.

Jonathan and I volunteered to make pancakes in the morning with the correct ingredients.

125

We never did.

Because we ran out of flour, we couldn't make the gnocchi, so Tina cooked up some pasta.

Paolo was helping his sister move, so he did not return home in time for dinner. We were disappointed because that meant we would have to wait to give Paolo his books.

Jonathan couldn't wait.

During dinner Jonathan told Tina of our flea market adventure and what we bought for Paolo.

She was hysterical with laughter.

We gave her the Charlie Brown book. She laughed and was so happy about the collection of comics that reminded her of the comics she read when she was a little girl. The ones that taught her about the American way of life.

We passed the time sharing our adventure to Cecina with Tina.

Tina was delighted to be a part of our adventure, and she reveled in sharing with us, her Italy.

Italian Chianti makers (19th century)

Chapter 17
Una band Americana!

Picking olives was the agenda for this Monday morning.

We had a light breakfast and we walked to the fields. Paolo was already there waiting for us.

We picked for about three hours, and then Paolo taught us the art of pruning the olive trees.

Most of the olives had been harvested.

Now it was time to complete the harvest season and prepare for the winter.

Because Paolo would be busy plowing the fields and planting, he gave us the chore of pruning the olive trees, on our own. It was challenging, but we did a pretty good job.

After lunch, our only chore was to pick three olive trees in front of the living quarters. Jonathan and I decided to complete the task so we could have the rest of the afternoon free.

After we finished, we got cleaned up and headed for town to get some snacks at the grocery store. While we were there we saw some children "Trick or Treating" in costume. Somehow, because we were in Italy, it seemed really cute.

There were also some people shooting off fireworks in one of the parking lots.

There was going to be a Halloween party in Ponteginori at our local bar later, so Jonathan and I decided to come back to town right after dinner.

Remember, this is Italy, so dinner did not start until eight-fifteen.

When we returned to the bar, to our surprise, it was overflowing with people.

A Barber was there giving people shaves with a straight edge razor and he brought in an old-fashioned barber chair, similar the ones we had in the states.

We ordered our drinks and tried to blend in.

We did not.

There was no place to sit and be less conspicuous, so we stood at the bar which made it even more obvious that we were not part of the local crowd.

Just about ten fifteen people started leaving, so some seats became available.

They served some cold cuts and bread, and the band was returning from their break.

It was a three-man band and the singer had an amazing voice. They were playing American music, singing in English which for the most part made them sound American. But they spoke Italian in between sets.

Jonathan and I wondered if they understood the lyrics of the songs they were singing. I was sure they did!

They performed a wide variety of American classics, including songs by Sting, Elton Jonathan, The Beatles, Maroon Five, Phil Collins and many more. They were quite good and Jonathan and I enjoyed listening to them.

Jonathan flirted with some of the young girls there, and we all had a good time.

He later told me that the girls were curious as to why he was at a bar with his father. So much for my blending in.

Although I was glad to be there, to have experienced the party-life of small-town Italy, I was out of my comfort zone.

I was surrounded by people but I felt so all alone.

Italian Street vendors in the East Village, NYC

Chapter 18
Com'e emozionante!

Today, we were going back to Cecina, with Tina!
What a great little city!

Cecina was destroyed during World War II, but after its reconstruction it gained popularity thanks to its clear, deep-blue water.

Cecina was a lively town that had a Centro lined with shops and cafes. It also has a very large train station which makes it accessible to the major cities.

Between Cecina's ancient center and its marina there is a tree-lined avenue stretching about three kilometers.

I loved Cecina!

Tina drove us to the Centro where there were hundreds of street vendors selling a wide variety of products. Clothing, coats, shoes, handbags just to mention a few. I resumed my quest for socks.

There was also a wide variety of food vendors selling fruits, vegetables, meats, fish, and cheese.

Tina bought lots of cheese and vegetables, and we had a great time walking through the streets shopping.

No children's socks! I bought some for my two oldest grandchildren, but there were no small sizes.

When we got back to the farm Tina prepared lunch.

After lunch she told us that Paolo would like us to continue to prune some of the olive trees.

Tina was anxious, because she had a lot of cooking to do to prepare for some guests that were arriving.

Jonathan and I offered to help, and she said, "that would be wonderful," and told us that after we were finished pruning, we should come to the kitchen to help her around five o'clock.

Jonathan and I took a short lunch break and headed for the olive tree grove around two thirty.

We were both very nervous about pruning the trees. We didn't want to cut off too many branches, but we also wanted to make sure that we did accomplish some pruning.

It was a slow process and we decided that it was better to cut less, rather than cut some good olive bearing branches.

We finished around four-thirty, took showers and headed for the kitchen to help Tina.

Jonathan helped making pumpkin flan, and I cut up some cheese and helped peal apples for apple pie.

When her guests arrived, Tina invited Jonathan and I to stay and have some wine with them.

They did not speak much English, so Tina translated for us. We served the flan, and everyone enjoyed it.

They were a young couple who were visiting from Northern Italy. They lived in an area near the Alps, and talked about how much snow they would get. They said the snow in the streets could get as high as ten feet tall. They loved to ski, and told us of their skiing adventures in the Alps.

With all the commotion in the kitchen, Tina did not have time to prepare anything for dinner, so we just ate some cheese and bread after her guests left.

Tina promised to take us to the Frantoio tomorrow. That is where they processed the olives for olive oil.

Jonathan and I were very excited about visiting the production facility.

Areas of travels

Chapter 19
Oh bene!

I woke up early the next morning.

I made some notes in my journal and put on my jeans.

Ahhh, to be putting on clean clothes in the morning, how refreshing!

I heard Jonathan walking around, so I went out to greet him in the kitchen area.

He said he received a text message from Tina that Paolo needed our help at nine o'clock.

Here we go again!

I changed into my work clothes and headed off to breakfast.

Breakfast was light this morning. Tea and toast. The funny thing about Tina is that the food she serves does not have to be piping hot.

She drinks her little cup of espresso after it's been sitting for five or ten minutes.

The toast is never hot enough to even melt the butter.

The tea however, was hot.

It was a simple, yet delightful breakfast of tea with honey, toast, cookies and biscuits.

Some mornings Tina would put out some granola cereal and yogurt and two hard boiled eggs. One for Jonathan and one for me. Eggs were not her typical breakfast item to serve but because we had previously spoken how American breakfasts usually consisted of eggs, she was being accommodating to us. That was the sweet nature of Tina.

During breakfast Tina told us that Paolo did not need our help in the field, but that he would like us to continue our tree pruning project.

We asked her if we were still going to visit the Frantoio. She said, "Of course we are, we will do that at three."

Off to the grove!

We did about two and a half hours of pruning and stopped for lunch.

For lunch Tina made more lasagna. Still no red sauce. Delicious, none the less!

Right after lunch we took off for the Frantoio.

It was only about a twenty-minute drive.

It was a very small place.

The building that housed the equipment was small and had three production lines.

There was a bin outside the building where they dumped the olives. The olives were then rolled onto a conveyor belt which climbed up to an opening at the top of the building where the olives were dumped into another bin inside the building. From there, the olives were shuffled again, removing most of the leaves and branches and washed. Then another beltway carried them into the press.

The press was an enclosed tank and we couldn't see what was going on. There the olives were pressed, and the oil was then sent through a hose into a holding tank.

Some farmers waited for their oil and took it home in metal canisters. Others, who wanted the oil bottled, left it there.

138

The oil was then transferred to a holding tank until the oil could be bottled. This process could take a few weeks.

It wasn't as intricate a process as I thought it would be. I guess I was expecting something more like an attraction at Disneyland, but it was good to see where the magic happens.

Lucca, Italy

Chapter 20
Andiamo!

The next day was pretty much business as usual.

Pruning the trees in the morning, lunch break, pruning in the afternoon, and then dinner.

Tina had ordered some movies from Amazon.com, and after dinner we watched Butch Cassidy and the Sundance Kid. She loves the movies from the sixties and seventies.

She said we should visit another city Friday afternoon since it would be our last day at the farm.

Friday morning at breakfast Tina said Jonathan and I should go to Lucca. A small city by Pisa. She said it was very beautiful there.

We said, "OK" and asked her when we should go, and she said around one o'clock. Then she said maybe we should go earlier. By the time breakfast was over our plan was to leave at eleven.

We pruned for about an hour and a half, showered and headed off to Lucca.

I was getting to be quite the Italian driver. Maneuvering the narrow winding roads, passing slower vehicles, and finding my way to the various cities.

Lucca was about an hour and a half drive from the farm, so we arrived there around twelve-thirty.

Lucca is a city on the Serchio River. It is known for the well-preserved Renaissance walls encircling its historic city center and its cobblestone streets.

Tree lined pathways are popular for strolling and cycling.

The city is surrounded by thick and high fortifications that date back to the Middle Ages. The jagged walls were designed by Leonardo Da Vinci.

We stopped at the first piazza, which was very small and had a slice of Pizza and a glass of wine. We were off to a very good start.

We decided to limit ourselves to just one slice so we could sample other pizzerias.

The Torre Guinigi was one of the many towers in the city. It was very tall, and there are trees at the top. Jonathan had to go up the stairs to the top, I stayed at the bottom and took his picture when he got there.

Lucca was so nice, lots of high-end shops along the main via. A lot of the shops were closed, and the streets were not very crowded because it was off-season.

We bought some chocolates to bring to Tina. We had a few for ourselves to sample first.

We found another pizzeria and sampled another slice.

All in all, it was another great excursion, filled with history, culture and good food!

On the way home, we stopped in Ponteginori to have a beer and say goodbye to our new friends.

We arrived back home and had a nice dinner with Tina and Paolo.

We gave them the gifts we bought for them in Lucca. The chocolates, a bottle of Sambuca, and the three-pack DVD of Il Padrino (The Godfather).

Paolo, like most Italians do not like to talk about the Mafia and the underworld. Paolo told us that the Mafia is a very real thing, back in the day, but primarily in Sicily. When we spoke of the movie, The Godfather, Paolo expressed interest, as he had never seen any of the movies.

The gifts were a big hit with Tina and Paolo.

Time for bed.

My plan was to pack in the morning and head to Florence to spend the night before my flight on Sunday.

No sightseeing.

Just chill at the hotel and enjoy fresh sheets and clean towels.

I was looking forward to getting home.

My time at the farm had been an enjoyable experience. Jonathan and I had learned so much about Italy, and farming, and they enjoyed having us to help them with their task of harvesting.

Our sharing about our traditions and culture was appreciated and they yearned to learn of what the U.S. was really like.

They said they would like to travel to the U.S. one day. Paolo particularly wanted to go to Durango and ride horses and hang out with the cowboys in the saloon.

My hope is that I was able to portray a proper image of Americans to the Italian people that came across my path. My desire was that I gave a good impression and some understanding of how people lived in America. So that, through my visit, they would have respect and love for the American people.

To have them know that we are, like Italy, a country of loving, hospitable people. That they could expect to be treated by

143

Americans with warmth and hospitality.

I trust that they felt that they would be treated by Americans the same way Americans are welcomed and treated in Italy.

San Gimignano

Chapter 21
E 'stato un piacere di conoscere tutti voi!

I will never forget how the sun burst into my window every morning to wake me.

The crisp air when I walked out of my cabin to greet the sun.

The mountains and the valleys just waiting for me to absorb their enormity and beauty.

I will always remember how I never tired of the views. Every turn on every road was a masterpiece to be admired.

Toscana, what a wonderful place to be!

But this morning I was awakened by the wind, and the dark dreary sky just waiting to unload its fill of rain.

I packed my bags and headed to Tina's table to have a light breakfast and say my goodbyes.

I shared with her what a wonderful experience it was to stay with them. I thanked her for their warmth and hospitality.

She thanked Jonathan and me for enlightening her of our American ways.

She loved the positive American spirit and how encouraging that was to her.

We took some photos with her and Paolo and I bid adieu!

Arriverderci Tina!

Arriverderci Paolo!

Arriverderci Jonathan!

Arriverderci Toscana!

All the months of preparation and anticipation of this adventure, and now it was all over. I have lived my entire life in compliance with the rules. I have always tried to live up to expectations of my Dad, of my teachers in school, of my wife, and of my children.

I never drifted from the plan to pursue my hearts desires, or to pursue my dreams.

It took me sixty-three years but in 2016, I finally took that leap of faith, and it paid off in spades! I had returned to Italy. The home of my ancestors. The core of who I am. An American who is 100% Italian. A heritage so rich, and full, that I wonder how I could ever have missed it?

I will always cherish this time and take with me the things I've learned.

The importance of embracing my heritage, passing it on to my children and grandchildren.

That I should be proud of being the grandson of Italian immigrants. Poor, uneducated people with no particular skills who risked it all for a better life. A better life not for them, but for their family and their descendants.

In retrospect I am not certain what that journey was really about. I yearned to find my heritage, my Italian roots. Was that the real journey though? I spent quality time in Italy traveling the regions, learning about the history and the Italian people. There are so many things I learned from that experience that have changed me.

I have come to the conclusion that this was really a journey of the discovery of me. To find myself, the person I lost so many years ago. It took losing my wife to begin that search, and get in touch with who I really am. This journey of discovery made me realize that I was a man full of emotions and feelings. A dreamer, a person so full of hope and faith that I believed I could accomplish anything I set my mind to. I lost touch with myself. I got wrapped up in all the chaos and the responsibility of life, taking care of my wife and my family.

Although I am still that person who lives my life responsibly, I have evolved to be that person that hopes and dreams. A man capable of deep loving relationships filled with emotion.

I know now that my relationships must change. I want to be a stronger Father to my children. I want to be able to share my emotions with them and help them on their journey of discovery. I must be a memorable Grandfather to my grandchildren, passing on to them the importance of relationships with their families and more importantly their relationship with God.

Frantoio Olive Tree

Epilogue
Grazie mille!

Grazie Nonno Domenico, grazie Nonno Enrico, for all that you did for the good of your family.

Thank you for leaving your homeland and your family for a promise called America.

Thank you for coming to America with no money, no home, no career path!

What courage! All in hopes of providing a better life for your family.

Your hopes and dreams have been truly realized in the fruit of your loins. Just two generations later your family has been blessed by the legacy you have left here in America.

I am proud to be the Italian you hoped I would be, living and prospering in America. That was your dream fulfilled!

I am proud of my Italian heritage and the country and people I can call my family!

Traditional Pizza

Come ti chiami?

Tina – Owner of Fattoria de Statiano

Paolo – Owner of Fattoria de Statiano

Jonathan – WOOF'r

Gordo – Beige Cat Leader

Tripod – Grey three-legged cat

Nike – Black Cat picked on by the other cats

Christina – Cleaning woman at Fattoria de Statiano

Raffaella – Tina's cousin

Enrico – Bartender at Betti's bar

Matteo – Bartender at Betti's bar

Barbara – Woman at the bar who spoke good English

Marco – Guest at Fattoria de Statiano

Deborah – Guest at Fattoria de Statiano

Cosa vuole dire?
Sono un italiano! – I am an Italian!

La creazione! - The beginning!

Un uomo grasso! - The fat man!

Non parlo Italiano! - I don't speak Italian!

Incredibile! - Incredible, unbelievable!

Buona notte! - Good night!

Grazie a Dio! - Thank God!

Che Stupido! - How stupid / What a fool!

Ero un po' deluso! - I was a little disappointed!

Arrivederci amico mio! - Goodbye my friend!

Benvenuti a casa, Jonathan! - Welcome home, Jonathan!

Momma mia! - Oh boy!

Fantastico! - Fantastic!

Era una giornata indaffarata! - It was a busy day!

Sogni D'oro! - Sweet dreams!

Una band Americana! - An American band!

Com'e emozionante! - How exciting!

Oh bene! - Oh boy!

Andiamo! - Let's go!

E' stato un piacere di conoscere tutti voi! - It was a pleasure to know all of you!

Grazie mille! - Thanks so much!

A canal in Venice

Note on images:

The images contained in this book were obtained from Wikipedia except for the map on page 152 which is from an Italian governement map.

For more information on WWOOF/Woofing and Tina and Paolo's farm please look up:

https://agriturismostatiano.com/en/about-us/